Following
Jesus with
Luke

Following Jesus with Luke

STONECROFT

HARVEST HOUSE PUBLISHERS
EUGENE, OREGON

Cover by Koechel Peterson & Associates, Inc., Minneapolis, Minnesota

Cover photo © iStockphoto / Thinkstock

FOLLOWING JESUS WITH LUKE
Stonecroft Bible Studies
Copyright © 2013 by Stonecroft Ministries, Inc.
Published by Harvest House Publishers
Eugene, Oregon 97402
www.harvesthousepublishers.com

    ISBN 978-0-7369-5262-0 (pbk.)
    ISBN 978-0-7369-5263-7 (eBook)

Printed in the United States of America

12 13 14 15 16 17 18 19 20 / VP-CD / 10 9 8 7 6 5 4 3 2 1

Contents

Acknowledgments

Stonecroft wishes to acknowledge and thank Janice Mayo Mathers for her dedication in serving the Lord through Stonecroft. Speaker, author, and member of the Board of Directors, Jan is the primary author of revised Stonecroft Bible Studies. We appreciate her love for God's Word and her love for people who need Him. Stonecroft also thanks the team who prayed for Jan, and those who edited, designed, and offered their creative input to make these studies accessible to all.

Welcome to
Stonecroft Bible Studies!

At Stonecroft, we connect you with God, each other, and your communities.

It doesn't matter where you've been or what you've done—God wants to be in relationship with you. And one place He tells you about Himself is in His Word—the Bible. Whether the Bible is familiar or new to you, its contents will transform your life and bring answers to your biggest questions.

Gather with people in your communities—women, men, couples, young and old alike—and discover together what the Bible says about the life of Jesus through the writer and historian Luke. As you read these accounts written by a man who talked to eyewitnesses and thoroughly investigated the events, you will find out more about who Jesus Christ is and what He does. And you'll see how His love and friendship can transform you from the inside out.

Each chapter of *Following Jesus with Luke* includes discussion questions to stir up meaningful conversation, specific Scripture verses to investigate, and time for prayer to connect with God and each other.

Discover more of God and His ways through this small-group exploration of the Bible.

Tips for Using This Study

This book has several features that make it easy to use and helpful for your life:

- The page number or numbers given after every Bible reference are keyed to the page numbers in the *Abundant Life Bible*. This handy paperback Bible uses the New Living Translation, a recent version in straightforward, up-to-date language. We encourage you to obtain a copy through your group leader or at stonecroft.org.

- Each chapter ends with a section called "Thoughts, Notes, and Prayer Requests." Use this space for notes or for thoughts that come to you during your group time or study, as well as prayer requests.

- In the back of the book you will find "Journal Pages"—a space available for writing down how the study is changing your life or any other personal thoughts, reactions, and reflections.

- Please make this book and study your own. We encourage you to use it and mark it in any way that helps you grow in your relationship with God!

If you find this study helpful, you may want to investigate other resources from Stonecroft. Please take a look at "Stonecroft Resources" in the back of the book or online at stonecroft.org/store.

> stonecroft.org

Introducing
Luke's Account of Jesus

Welcome to the Stonecroft Bible Study *Following Jesus with Luke*. This story of the life of Christ, from the perspective of one of His followers, gives us the opportunity to see Jesus as both God and Man, as the promised Savior.

Luke is one of the four Gospels that make up the first four books of the New Testament: Matthew, Mark, Luke, and John. Each of the authors, under the inspiration of the Holy Spirit (2 Timothy 3:16, page 915), wrote his account of Jesus' life for a different reason, and naturally emphasized different things:

- Matthew, a disciple, wrote to the Jews and included many Old Testament Scripture references. He presented Jesus as the Messiah, the Sovereign King, and frequently called Him the Son of David and the Son of God.

- Mark wrote to the Romans and presented Christ as the perfect Servant of God, doing the work that God gave Him to do.

- John, another disciple, presented Christ as the Son of God and emphasized His divinity.

- Luke, a Gentile, wrote to the Gentiles (people not of Jewish heritage), emphasizing both the divinity and humanity of Christ. He frequently called Him by the same name Jesus called Himself—the Son of Man.

- The Gospel of Luke is believed to have been written around AD 60. Like the other Gospels, it is an accurate, historical account of the life of Jesus. Luke, as an educated writer, used various styles, including literary and classical as well as more everyday ones. His account is also the longest and the most complete biography of Jesus. Nearly half of its material is not included in the other reports of the life of Christ. For example:

- There are 14 parables found in Luke that are not in the other Gospels.

- Of the 21 miracles described in Luke, 7 are exclusive to this book.

- Six of the prayers of Jesus are recorded only in this Gospel.

There are many things to learn and discover within the pages of this wonderful book of the Bible, written by a man who dedicated himself to recording an accurate account of the life of Jesus Christ. And while we cannot cover every passage thoroughly, this study endeavors to capture the essence of the life of Jesus as reflected by Luke. Because Luke faithfully served God with what he had, his life and writings have been a source of blessing and encouragement for centuries. May you also be blessed and encouraged as you go through this exciting study.

Outline of the Book of Luke

	Preparation	Early Ministry	Teaching Ministry	Sacrifice and Resurrection
Chapters	1–3	4, 5–8	9–19	19–23, 24
Time	First 30 years	First year and second year	Third year	8 days 40 days
Location	Nazareth	Galilee	Judea and Perea*	Jerusalem
	Obscurity	Miracles	Parables	The Great Miracle

---

* Perea was the name of the region on the east side of the southern half of the Jordan River—that is, northeast of the Dead Sea.

1

Announcement of Jesus

I t was an ordinary day. The sun peeked up over the eastern hori-
zon—just as it always did. The rooster's crow awakened her—just
as it always did. As usual, her very first thought was of Joseph.
Joseph! She was so happy to be engaged to him. For a few extra
moments she lingered beneath the warmth of her blankets, daydream-
ing about the future. First, of course, the wedding—oh, how she'd
imagined *that* day—and then would come babies...

The sound of her mother rustling around drew her reluctantly
from her bed. As usual, there was much work to be done and her
mother needed her help. After dressing, she went outside to enjoy a
few moments of solitude before the day began in earnest. The sky was
not fully light, and this in-between time was her favorite part of day.

Suddenly, a movement caught her eye. Well, not a movement
exactly, more of a feeling maybe. Mary looked around in puzzlement,
sensing something she couldn't define. Her skin tingled, and even
though she didn't feel chilled, she pulled her cloak tightly around her
shoulders.

Mary!

She whirled around at the sound of her name, her whole body
alert and trembling. *And there he stood.* Although she'd never seen one
before, she knew instinctively this was an angel. Her heart pounded

in fear and wonder. Without another word being spoken, her life had just veered off its ordinary course...

Prayer

    God, your Word is alive and powerful. It is sharper than the sharpest two-edged sword, cutting between soul and spirit, between joint and marrow. As I go through this study, may you reveal my innermost thoughts and desires. Help me to come boldly before you, knowing that you will give me mercy and grace when I need it most (Hebrews 4:12,16, page 922).

Mary's life was forever changed that day when she encountered one of God's angels. She would give birth to Jesus, the Son of the Most High, who would reign forever and whose Kingdom would have no end. Luke recorded all of this in his Gospel (Luke 1:31-33, page 779).

Luke and His Purpose for Writing

Before looking further into Jesus Christ's birth, let's first find out more about the author Luke himself. Turn to Colossians 4:14 (page 904), and note his occupation.

Did you notice the adjective used to describe Luke? *Beloved* doctor. That one word tells us a great deal about him, doesn't it? His profession also explains why he used medical terms in his writing. Luke worked closely with the apostle Paul, who was an early Christian missionary. Both were well-educated men who pursued spiritual as well as intellectual growth, which may explain their close friendship.

Luke, a Gentile contributor to the Bible, joined Paul on his second missionary journey and traveled with him most of the time from then on. In fact, when Paul was in prison (2 Timothy 4:11, page 916), he stayed with him as his personal companion and physician. God led Luke every step of the way as he collected facts and interviewed eyewitnesses, preparing him to eventually write two books of the Bible: Luke and Acts (which is confirmed by the writings of historians and by the Muratorian canon of the second century). God specifically gave him a desire to pursue truth, along with the skills needed to perform in his profession as a doctor.

What unique gifting and strengths has God given you?

writing

How might you use them to benefit others?

encouragement

Read Luke 1:1-4 (page 779).
What resources did Luke use to write his account?

Carefully-investigated eyewitness accounts and believers' (servants') words

Why did Luke write this Gospel?

so Theophilus' understanding of the gospel might be reinforced — an easy, chronilogical account

Both of the books Luke wrote were addressed to Theophilus, whose identity is not known. There are two schools of thought regarding him. One is based in the fact that Theophilus was both a common name and a title of honor among educated Romans and Jews. It means "lover of God" or "friend of God," so Luke could have used this as a general address to Christians. The second thought is that

Luke was addressing a specific person, and since Luke referred to him as "most honorable" Theophilus, he was most likely a Roman official of some sort.

Zechariah and the Angel

Now let's see where Luke's wonderful account begins. Read Luke 1:5-10 (page 779).

In the Old Testament, we read that God chose the descendants of Moses' brother, Aaron, to be priests in the Temple. Later, King David divided the priests into 24 groups (1 Chronicles 24:1-19, page 327), and each priest took his turn officiating at the Temple. On the day that Luke is writing about, it is Zechariah's turn to officiate (Exodus 30:7, page 68). As he is going about his duties something truly stunning occurs. Read Luke 1:11-12.

Can you imagine what Zechariah's thoughts must have been when he looked up and saw an angel standing near the incense altar? Angel sightings were an almost unknown occurrence in Zechariah's day. In fact, it had been more than 400 years since God had sent a messenger to speak directly to any of His people. No wonder Zechariah was shaken and overwhelmed with fear.

Pretend that you were Zechariah. How would you have reacted?

stunned — speechless —
"brain-spin"

What are the two first statements that the angel says to Zechariah in verse 13?

* DON'T BE AFRAID
* YOUR PRAYERS WERE HEARD

Those were two very important messages Zechariah needed to hear. Then the angel's next words were to prove life-changing, and they might have been just as hard for Zechariah to believe as was the fact he was seeing an angel.

What do you learn about God from the three distinct messages the angel spoke to Zechariah?

GOD IS VERY MUCH INTERESTED IN US AS INDIVIDUALS — HE IS INTIMATELY RELATED & INVOLVED IN OUR LIVES

Why did Zechariah struggle with what the angel had just told him? See verse 18.

THE ANGEL'S MESSAGE CONTRADICTS "NORMAL"/LOGICAL EXPERIENCE

Just imagine receiving such news when it has been what you and your spouse have longed for, prayed for, hoped for—for many, many years. However, that was back when you were younger, when all your friends were having children. Now your friends are having grandkids! Your hope of ever becoming parents had long ago been put to rest.

God's timing on answering prayer is sometimes questionable from our perspective, isn't it? Describe a time when God's timing in answering your prayers didn't quite line up with what you had in mind.

The four verses following the angel's incredible news must have sent Zechariah's head into an even greater spin. Read verses 13-17 and note all the specifics the angel told him about the son they were to name John.

- ANSWER TO PRAYER
- ELIZABETH WOULD BEAR HIS (BIOLOGICAL) SON
- ALREADY NAMED: JOHN
- (JOHN) WILL BRING JOY TO THEM & MANY (OTHERS)
- WILL BE GREAT IN GOD'S SIGHT
- MUST REFRAIN FROM WINE & FERMENTED DRINKS
- FILLED WITH HOLY SPIRIT FROM MOTHER'S WOMB
- WILL TURN HEARTS OF MANY BACK TO GOD
- IN "SPIRIT OF ELIJAH" WILL PREPARE WAY FOR "MESSIAH"

What questions or doubts would you have after the angel listed all of these specifics about your future son?

- why my son ?!
- how can I be sure (John) doesn't stray from this course ?!
- will this bring lots of attention to us ?

Read verses 19-22. What was the result of Zechariah's disbelief?

he was made mute / couldn't speak

The Great News Is Announced to Mary

Now read Luke 1:26-38 (pages 779-780).

Luke apparently obtained the detailed information surrounding the birth of Jesus from Mary herself, because he even writes about her thoughts at times. But remember, he had at least two years to research and interview people while Paul was imprisoned in the region of Judea (Acts 24–25, pages 852-854). Can you imagine how moving it would have been to interview Mary and hear the miraculous details from her perspective?

Let's compare and contrast Mary's and Zechariah's experiences with the angel Gabriel.

What are the similarities between Gabriel's greetings to Mary and Zechariah?

- UNEXPECTED APPEARANCE OF ANGEL/GABRIEL
- "DON'T BE AFRAID"
- SPECIFIC, DETAILED ANNOUCEMENT (S)

How was Mary's reaction to Gabriel different from Zechariah's?

- IMMEDIATE SURRENDER/OBEDIENCE/BELIEF

What is the role of Elizabeth's son, John (verses 16-17)?

RE-ESTABLISH THE PEOPLES' HEARTS FOR GOD ___ PREPARE THE WAY (MAKE PEOPLE AWARE) FOR THE COMING MESSIAH (JESUS)

What is Jesus' role? Read Luke 1:32-33, and list the five messages concerning Christ that Gabriel tells Mary.

1. JESUS WILL BE GREAT

2. CALLED "SON OF THE MOST HIGH"

3. GOD WILL GIVE HIM "FATHER" DAVID'S THRONE (ISRAEL)

4. JESUS WILL REIGN OVER HOUSE OF JACOB (ISRAEL) FOREVER

5. JESUS' KINGDOM WILL NEVER END

What was Mary's reaction to Gabriel's message (verses 34,38)?

- HOW? (VIRGIN BIRTH) ASTONISHMENT
- OKAY — LET IT BE — "I AM THE LORD'S SERVANT" (OBEDIENCE/ACCEPTANCE)

The God of the Impossible

In verse 36, Mary finds out that her relative Elizabeth is also pregnant. Why do you think God had Gabriel specifically mention Elizabeth's pregnancy to Mary?

- A MIRACLE IS ALSO HAPPENING WITH SOMEONE (ELIZ.) KNOWN TO MARY (SOMETHING SHE COULD VERIFY)
- IF POSSIBLE WITH ELIZ. THEN MUST BE FOR MARY, TOO (AND SHOWS GOD KNOWS ALL-THINGS)

Elizabeth finally was pregnant after years of being barren and past the age of having children. Mary, on the other hand, was extremely young and was a virgin. Both women experienced divine intervention in their lives—they were witnesses to the fact that *"nothing is impossible with God"* (verse 37).

God is all-powerful. His Word will come true whether it seems possible or not. What is the significance of this statement?

HE IS ALL-POWERFUL AND CAN BE FULLY TRUSTED (THE REMAINING, UNFULFILLED PROPHECIES IN SCRIPTURE WILL COME TO PASS!).

Can you think of a time when you have seen God do the impossible in someone's life? Please explain.

Is there a situation in your life today in which you want God to intervene and do something impossible from our perspective? Describe it briefly.

Now share it with God. He knows your thoughts and understands your feelings. Ask Him to help you fully embrace the powerful truth of this verse, and continue to pray for His will to be done in the situation. Remember, the good that God has for us—His good, perfect, and pleasing will—will always be better than the "good" we may desire. Romans 8:28 (page 863) says that He "*causes everything to work together for the good of those who love God and are called according to his purpose for them,*" so spend your time and energy on loving God, and then He will work out the impossibilities for good—the good that is so good, only He can conceive of it.

The impossible happened when the Holy Spirit came upon Mary, a virgin, and then nine months later she gave birth to Jesus, the holy Son of God. This virgin birth was impossible without God's intervention. It was also necessary to fulfill God's prophecy in the Old Testament about the Savior's birth. The account of Jesus' birth in Matthew 1:22-23 (page 733) explicitly states that His virgin birth from Mary was a direct fulfillment of what the Lord spoke through the prophet Isaiah: "*All right then, the Lord himself will give you the sign. Look! The virgin will conceive a*

The virgin birth of Jesus is a critical part in God's plan for our redemption. From the day we are born we are on a journey toward death and separation from God because of our sinful nature that has been brought on through Adam's sin in the Garden of Eden (Romans 5:12, page 860). But through God's immense love for us and in His desire to have relationship with us, He sent His Son, Jesus, to be born of a virgin. Jesus was fully God, yet He was fully man. As God, Jesus had the power to redeem sinners. He himself was sinless. He was willing to die for our sins. He willingly bridged the gap between God and us when He paid the penalty of death for us. That incredible, inconceivable act of love made it possible for us to have a personal relationship with God. Jesus' birth, death, and resurrection mean that when we acknowledge and accept the price Jesus paid for us, we will no longer be under the penalty of death. We have the assurance of eternal life with God.

child! She will give birth to a son and will call him Immanuel (which means 'God is with us')" (Isaiah 7:14, page 522).

The Blessing of God

Almost immediately after hearing from the angel Gabriel, Mary left to visit her relative Elizabeth, who at the time was more than six months pregnant with John the Baptist. Read Luke 1:39-45 (page 780).

What happened when Mary greeted Elizabeth?

Baby (John) leaped for joy within Elizabeth's womb

How did Elizabeth know that Mary was pregnant with her Lord (verse 41)?

Elizabeth was filled with the Holy Spirit

Why did Elizabeth say Mary was blessed? How can this be significant for your life?

Mary was serving as a vessel in God's service — it is a true blessing to serve the Lord

Since Mary and Elizabeth were relatives, they had always known each other, but they were from different generations, and their relationship would have reflected that. Suddenly, they are now sharing similar, unique experiences:

• They both experience great shame—Elizabeth through

her inability to conceive (which was a tremendous shame in that culture), and Mary, through her pregnancy before marriage.

- They both experience a miraculous pregnancy.
- Their unborn children both have great destinies.

No other woman alive could possibly understand the turn their lives had taken. They must have drawn tremendous comfort and encouragement from each other at this meeting and throughout the rest of their lives.

But there's something else that must have been very comforting to Mary in this meeting with Elizabeth. Remember, the angel had appeared only to her—not to her parents and not to Joseph (at least not yet—see Matthew 1:18-25, page 733). So as far as anyone knew, Mary was pregnant and unmarried—an offense worthy of death in her culture. Not just her reputation was at stake, but also her life! Do you think she had questions after her encounter with the angel? Do you think she ever questioned her sanity? Imagine trying to convince her parents that even though she was still a virgin, she was nonetheless pregnant. As her parent, would you have believed her?

Look at Luke 1:42-45 again. What was Elizabeth's response to Mary's visit?

Joy — excitement — a shared relief & understanding from their unique, mutual circumstances

Can you imagine the immense relief and reassurance Mary must have felt when Elizabeth acknowledged her divine pregnancy? How good of God to immediately lead her to visit the only woman in the entire world who would understand and recognize what had happened to her!

Mary's response to Elizabeth's reaction is obvious in verses 46-55. This song of praise is called the "Magnificat" (which is the first word of the song in Latin). Can you hear the joy in Mary's voice? She is with someone who recognizes and verifies her experience. She can fully release the emotions she's held tightly within her and celebrate this incredible occurrence. What a joyful, exuberant time these two women must have had together! They had each been singled out by God in such a miraculous way.

Who in your life can you be an encouraging voice to like Elizabeth was to Mary?

Mary stayed with Elizabeth for three months, leaving for her home in Nazareth just before Elizabeth was due to give birth (verse 56).

Read Luke 1:57-66 (page 780).
Don't you love the typical family drama this passage portrays? Everyone is weighing in on what the baby should be named. Have you ever been in a similar situation?

— no —

But — the people "made signs" to Zechariah ?!? ☺ (eventhough he could still hear!).

Elizabeth ignores the suggestions and announces, *"His name is John!"* It sets off instant protest. *"What?... There is no one in all your family by that name,"* they object, and a flurry of hand gestures is sent off in Zechariah's direction, who is still unable to speak and possibly unable to hear.

God Is Sending Salvation to His People

Immediately after Zechariah confirmed to the crowd that his son's name would be John, his voice returned and he began to prophesy. Read verses 67-80. Write all the encouraging and gratitude-filled phrases below.

- GOD OF ISRAEL HAS REDEEMED HIS PEOPLE
- RAISED UP "HORN" OF SALVATION IN HOUSE OF DAVID —ANSWER TO PROPHECY—
- SALVATION FROM ENEMIES
- REMEMBERED HIS HOLY COVENANT
- ENABLED PEOPLE TO SERVE (GOD) WITHOUT FEAR
- JOHN (PROPHET OF THE MOST HIGH) WILL PREPARE WAY FOR MESSIAH
- " WILL MAKE PEOPLE AWARE OF SINS & COMING SALVATION

Look back over your list. It's faith-inspiring, isn't it? God keeps His word; He never abandons us. Reread verses 76-79. What does Zechariah say that his child will be called, and what will he do?

- PROPHET OF THE MOST HIGH
- PREPARE WAY FOR MESSIAH
- MAKE PEOPLE AWARE OF THEIR SINS (RE-FOCUS THEM ON SPIRITUAL MATTERS)
- LET PEOPLE KNOW SALVATION — ANSWERED PROPHECY — IS ON ITS WAY

What a beautiful picture this prophecy paints! Can you envision this elderly man, who has spent his life in faithfulness to God, gazing in wonder at the brand-new miracle in his arms? Did you notice the precious message of salvation tucked within this passage? How does Zechariah say we will receive salvation?

THROUGH FORGIVENESS OF SINS — BY BEING LED FROM DARKNESS & SHADOW OF DEATH INTO THE LIGHT OF THE KNOWLEDGE OF SALVATION.

What an incredible first chapter! Two encounters with angels. Two miraculous pregnancies. And a God for whom nothing is impossible. If God can do all of this, is there anything He can't do for you?

As you reflect on all you've just read, hold your impossible circumstance out to God, and worship the One for whom nothing is impossible.

Personal Reflection and Application

From this chapter,

I see...

I believe...

I will...

Prayer

God, what a comfort to know that nothing is impossible for you. Your Word will always come true. I can give you all my worries and cares and know that you care for me and will work everything together for good—your good, perfect, and pleasing will—in my life, because I love you (Luke 1:37, page 780; 1 Peter 5:7, page 937; Romans 8:28, page 863).

———— *Thoughts, Notes, and Prayer Requests* ————

2

Jesus' Early Life

The man stifled a yawn as he leaned back against the rock, shifted his bad leg, and gazed up at the night sky. His eyes were heavy, but he didn't want to close them yet. He loved this time of night when the stars were at their brightest. Sometimes they seemed so close he couldn't stop himself from reaching upward, as if to touch them. The tiny lamb beside him nuzzled in closer. He was the runt of the litter and very likely wouldn't survive—but the shepherd wasn't ready to give up on him yet. He had a knack with cast-off animals like this one. Perhaps it was because he too had been cast off as a young child, abandoned by his parents because he was defective. But he had survived, in spite of his deformity—just as he was determined the little lamb beside him would survive.

Suddenly, the heavens filled with a blinding light. He lurched to his feet in terror. *What was happening?* He glanced around to where the other shepherds had been sleeping and saw they too were on their feet, shading their eyes from the blinding light. *Oh, Lord! What on earth—*

"Don't be afraid!" The shepherds all saw and heard the being at once. It had to be an angel, although none of them had ever seen one. "I bring you good news that will bring great joy to all people! The Savior has been born!"

Instantly, the sky was filled with a vast host of other angels—all praising God at once. It was the most beautiful, melodious sound the shepherd had ever heard. It made him want to weep and laugh all at once. It made him want to shout and whisper and dance and kneel. He stood mesmerized by their words, hope and wonder flooding through his body. *This was the Promised One he'd heard about his whole life—whose love had no limits, even for him, a cast-off.* He felt a warmth coursing through him, a feeling he'd never felt—of belonging, of acceptance, and of love.

He grabbed up the little lamb, and hobbling behind the other shepherds he hurried toward Bethlehem.

Prayer

Father, even though I wasn't present with the shepherds in that field more than 2000 years ago, I pray that I will still glorify and praise you for all that I have seen and heard in your Word about Jesus' coming to earth to be our Savior. May your Word take root in my life so I will grow in the grace and knowledge of our Lord and Savior Jesus Christ (Luke 2:20, page 781; 2 Peter 3:18, page 940).

Mary and Joseph Await Jesus' Birth

Mary and Joseph were living in Nazareth at the time Mary became pregnant (Luke 1:26, page 779). Now read Micah 5:2 (page 706). This verse is a prophecy about the birth of the *"Ruler of Israel,"* referring to Jesus. Where does it say He will be born?

So there's a problem, isn't there? Did the prophet Micah misunderstand the message God gave him? Did Mary and Joseph miss God's direction? Jesus is supposed to be born in Bethlehem, but Mary and Joseph are living in Nazareth. Details that seem impossible have the most incredible way of working themselves out, when God is in the picture.

As a Jew, Mary was familiar with all the prophecies surrounding the Messiah's birth. Do you suppose she wondered about this small detail? Do you suppose she and Joseph ever discussed it as her pregnancy progressed?

Have you had conversations in your house regarding matters you're tempted to take into your own hands?

> Mary and Joseph were living in Nazareth when notification of the census was given. Read Luke 2:1-6 (page 781). How did God resolve the issue of their place of residence?
>
> *Caesar Agustus called for a census to be taken, causing Joseph (& Mary) to travel to Bethlehem — because of Joseph's family line (w/ DAVID).*

Don't you love it? Who'd have thought of having the Roman Emperor himself get the young couple to the place they were supposed to be at the exact time they were supposed to be there? Only God, for whom nothing is impossible!

One other point of interest is the distance from Nazareth to Bethlehem. It is approximately 80 miles between the two cities.

Humble Circumstances

Verses 6 and 7 are beautifully simple: *"And while they were there, the time came for her baby to be born. She gave birth to her first child, a son. She wrapped him snugly in strips of cloth and laid him in a manger, because there was no lodging available for them."* The most miraculous event in history summed up in a handful of words!

The last part of verse 7 finds the little family without normal lodging, because the town is filled with people who are all there for the same reason—to be counted in the census. A Middle-Eastern inn in Bible times did not resemble our motels today. Some were merely small, crude resting places, such as caves. Other larger inns looked like fortresses, with an outer wall about 20 feet high. An arched gateway opened into a large, open court with a water source, where horses, camels, and baggage were placed. Around the wall was a platform of guest rooms. Travelers provided their own bedding, cooking utensils, and provisions.

Sometimes there were stables between the rear wall of the travelers' rooms and the outer wall. The platform on which the guest rooms were built projected into the stable, forming a ledge which was used as a manger. Some believe it was a manger such as this where Mary first laid her baby, but no one knows for certain. All we do know is what the Bible tells us: There was no lodging available, and Mary laid her baby in a manger.

Do you see any symbolism in the fact there was no room for Jesus? *EVEN MANKIND HAS TO INTENTIONALLY "MAKE ROOM" IN THEIR HEARTS FOR HIM.*

According to Isaiah 57:15 (page 562), where does God call home? *• A HIGH & HOLY PLACE and • WITH THE CONTRITE & LOWLY IN SPIRIT*

This verse shows an interesting juxtaposition, doesn't it? High and holy with contrite and humble. Why is this combination of terms significant? *HE SIMULTANEOUSLY (OMNISCIENT/OMNIPRESENT) LIVES IN HEAVEN AND IN THE HEARTS OF HIS BELIEVERS (WHO ALSO ARE "JUSTIFIED" UNTO HOLINESS.).*

The News Is Announced

Jesus' birth was a momentous occasion for all of history—so momentous that it has become a significant measurement of time almost worldwide: *BC.* Before Christ. The actual date of Jesus' birth is not known, but during the fourth century, the Roman emperor Constantine set December 25 as the day to commemorate His birth. Thus we have the holiday known as Christmas, celebrated all over the world by the exchanging of gifts.

Word of Jesus' birth spread quickly. Read Luke 2:8-12 (page 781). How was the first announcement made, and to whom was it made?

AN ANGEL APPEARED AND MADE THE ANNOUNCEMENT TO SHEPHERDS IN THE AREA.

Another angelic encounter! And another terrified audience! According to verse 10, what was the first thing the angel said?

DON'T BE AFRAID

The sudden appearance of an angel always seems to frighten people, but I think that's understandable, don't you? More important, God understands this fear. Each time, He has the angel immediately reassure the person. This is significant because it shows that He understands our tendency to be afraid. Throughout the Bible we read the phrase "Do not fear." Here are just a few references where God tells us there is no need to fear:

• Isaiah 41:10 (page 548)

I AM YOUR GOD; I WILL STRENGTHEN, HELP & UPHOLD YOU

- Luke 12:7 (page 794)

  ~~~ YOU ARE VALUABLE

- John 14:27 (page 824)

  ~~~ (I) GIVE YOU MY PEACE

Whatever we come up against in life, if we look to God, our fears will be calmed. Read Psalm 27:1-3 (page 425). The psalmist knows to put his trust in God. Verse 3 says, *"Even if I am attacked, I will remain confident."* There is an unexplainable peace that enters our heart when we set our mind on God rather than the circumstance. Read Philippians 4:6-7 (page 901).

Isn't that wonderful? When we give our fears over to God in prayer, His peace will guard our hearts and minds—in other words, He will protect our mind from debilitating fear. God understands your fears, and He wants to take your fear away. Hold out your fears to Him, and ask Him to replace them with greater trust in Him. Each time a fear returns, replace it immediately with a trust thought. Keep doing this, and before long, you will be amazed at what has happened within you. God will not disappoint you!

Now let's go back to the shepherds. Once the angel had assured them they had nothing to fear, what happened? Read Luke 2:13-14.
→ SUDDENLY A GREAT COMPANY OF ANGELS APPEARED
Don't you wonder what it must have been like in heaven as time drew near for Jesus' arrival on earth? How excited do you think the angels were, when at last they were able to enter the atmosphere of earth and fill the night sky with their heavenly radiance, gloriously worshipping God? Oh, what an amazing sight and sound that must have been!

I saw an incredible display of the northern lights when living in Alaska. It happened at midnight—the sky literally blazed to life with dancing colors that sometimes pulsed in blues and greens and then swayed with red and gold. It was so magnificent I could scarcely breathe.

Our sons were five and seven at the time. My husband and I woke them up and carried them outside so they could see the glorious display. We lay on the ground, and I kept saying, "Don't ever forget what you're seeing! Don't ever forget!" Sadly, all they remember now of the heavenly wonder is me telling them, "Don't ever forget!"

But even now, years later, I can close my eyes and see that blazing sky all over again—and there weren't even angels involved! Imagine seeing angels, hearing them worship God while the sky danced with brilliant light around them. Oh, what a glorious birth announcement to the world! Our Redeemer had left the splendor of heaven and arrived on earth as a newborn baby, so we could share fully in His inheritance. It's almost beyond comprehension, isn't it?

Read Luke 2:15-16 (page 781).
What happened when the angels returned to heaven?

THE SHEPHERDS BELIEVED AND WENT TO BETHLEHEM WHERE THEY FOUND MARY & BABY JESUS

What do you suppose Mary and Joseph thought when a motley band of shepherds suddenly showed up at the manger? Do you think the shepherds came running up, breathless with excitement? Or do you think they came tiptoeing in with reverence and awe? How would you have arrived?

• OUT-OF-BREATH FROM HURRYING, BUT THEN QUIET & HESITANT UPON ARRIVING (RELUCTANT TO INTERRUPT FAMILY'S PRIVACY).

What do you think their thoughts were as they gazed down at the helpless and oh-so-vulnerable baby? How do you think their minds processed the fact that this was the Savior they had read about in Holy Scripture? This was *God* in human form—just as He'd long ago promised (Isaiah 7:14, page 522). Apparently they had no doubts about what they were seeing, because what does Luke 2:17-20 (page 781) say they did next?

.THE SHEPHERDS WENT OUT AND SPREAD THE GOOD NEWS THEN RETURNED, PRAISING & GLORIFYING GOD (FOR ANSWERED PROPHECY — GOD'S FAITHFULNESS).

Look again at verse 19. What a picture this paints! Mary has just given birth to her first child. Her body is sore and exhausted; her emotions are tender. Her heart has just gone through an unparalleled transformation, enlarging itself to accommodate a new and massive love—the love of a mother for her child. *So many changes.* And remember, she knows what the Scriptures say about her child—not just about His birth, but also His future. So many things for this young mother to store in her heart—so many things for her to ponder.

Each of the last four verses contains a key phrase that illustrates a true Christmas celebration. You might want to underline them in your Bible:

- Verse 17: They told everyone. We need to tell everyone about Christ.

- Verse 18: They were astonished. We should never cease to be astonished by what God has done for us.

- Verse 19: She thought about them often. We should think often about the real meaning of Christmas.

- Verse 20: They were glorifying and praising God. We should glorify and praise God for what He has done for us.

If Christmas has lost its deeper meaning in your life, these four steps will restore the magnificence of this momentous holiday. It is worthy of our celebration!

The Infant Jesus in the Temple

Now read Luke 2:21-24. After 40 days had passed, Mary and Joseph traveled north of Bethlehem to Jerusalem where the Temple was. While there, they took care of three things that were required by Jewish law (Leviticus 12, page 87, and Exodus 13:2, page 53). They performed the ceremony of purification, they dedicated their baby to God, and they offered a sacrifice. While they were in the Temple, an amazing thing happened.

Read Luke 2:25-32.
Who was Simeon? A DEVOUT BELIEVER

What had the Holy Spirit revealed to Simeon?
SIMEON WOULD SEE THE PROMISED MESSIAH BEFORE HE (SIMEON) DIES

What did Simeon do when he saw Jesus in the Temple?
HE TOOK JESUS IN HIS ARMS AND PRAISED GOD

Can you imagine having someone take your child in his arms and rapturously praise God, saying that now he can die in peace, since he's seen your child?

So many things are at work here. God has led Simeon to the Temple at exactly the time Mary and Joseph are there. But I don't think this meeting is just for Simeon's sake. I think God arranged it for Mary and Joseph's sake as well. How frequently do you think they second-guessed themselves before and after Jesus' birth? Do you think they ever hesitantly asked each other as they gazed at their baby, "Can our son really, truly be the Messiah?"

God had chosen them to be the earthly parents of His Son. He knew what a stretch that assignment was for them. God brought people to them in the early days—everyday people whose lives were transformed—to confirm Jesus' deity. In addition to shepherds and wise men, there were Simeon and Anna, a woman we'll talk about soon. An important aspect of Simeon's worshipful words about Jesus is found in verse 32. As a *"light,"* what will Jesus do?

SALVATION WOULD BE REVEALED
TO GENTILES (AS WELL AS THE JEWS)

God had promised the Jews a *Messiah*—a Savior—but Simeon said that the salvation Jesus brought with him was for everyone—not just the Jews.

Now read verses 33-35. As a new mother, how would these words fall on your heart?

HEAVY ___ JOY - SHATTERING -
OMINOUS ___ SAD

The encounter with Simeon wasn't the only remarkable meeting in the Temple that day. A woman named Anna was there. She also recognized Jesus as the Messiah. Read Luke 2:36-40. What was her reaction?

ANNA APPROACHED THEM, SHE GAVE
THANKS TO GOD & SPOKE TO OTHERS
AROUND HER WHO WERE ANTICIPATING
THEIR MESSIAH.

Imagine if we shared her same level of excitement about Jesus! Imagine if we talked to everyone about Jesus. Even though a relationship with Jesus makes a dramatic difference in our lives, we may grow accustomed to the wonder of what He did

If you do not know about this transformative work, ask someone to share what Christ has done for them. You may also want to read the "Know God" section (pages 185–187) near the end of this book.

for us. Let's stop right now and ask God to reignite our passion and excitement for how Christ has transformed our lives.

Travelers from the East

At this point in Luke's account, he skips ahead to when Jesus was 12 and in the Temple again. But in Matthew's account we are told of another notable occurrence that took place after Jesus' birth. Apparently, Mary and Joseph had returned to Bethlehem when this happened, because it says they were living in a house there. At any rate, a group of men arrived in Jerusalem and went straight to the palace of King Herod because, as we will see, they were looking for a king. Where else would you expect to find a king but at a palace?

Read Matthew 2:1-8 (page 734).
What led the wise men to Jerusalem from their homes in the eastern lands?

HIS (SPECIAL) STAR IN THE EAST

What did they come to do?

TO WORSHIP HIM

What was King Herod's reaction to the wise men's visit?

TROUBLED / DISTURBED — HE SOUGHT COUNSEL w/ CHIEF PRIESTS & TEACHERS OF THE LAW TO FIND OUT MORE (PROPHETIC) INFORMATION — THEN HE REQUESTED THE MAGI FIND JESUS & THEN TELL WHERE HE COULD BE FOUND.

What do you think made the men believe that the moving star would lead them to a king? How did they sense there was something significant enough about this king that they wanted to come worship him? And how did these studiers of the stars know that the king they were looking for was a newborn baby? There are so many unanswered questions, aren't there? The only possible conclusion is that the Holy Spirit was at work, spreading the news of Jesus' birth in many creative ways, very possibly from Old Testament books taken into the captivity in Babylon (the eastern lands) by the Jews.

However these men from the east learned about the star that would lead them to newborn Jesus, their knowledge was, nonetheless, severely limited. They knew nothing about the political situation in King Herod's territory. As a result, they showed little diplomacy and no tact in approaching Herod with a question that seemed to be saying, "Where is the real king?" They didn't know their visit would cause a problem for the wicked king—but God knew and protected them. Through a dream, God warned the wise men not to return to Herod and to return to their country by another route. Let's read the rest of this story in Matthew 2:9-12 (page 734).

What presents did the visitors bring?

GOLD, INCENSE & MYRRH

Such extravagant gifts for a child, and yet they were very significant—and even prophetic. Gold was a gift for a king. Frankincense speaks of worship and sacrifice, and myrrh was used for anointing as well as for embalming. God kept confirming to Mary and Joseph that the child He had entrusted to them was truly the Son of God who came to save the world from sin.

God not only rescued the wise men from Herod, but He also rescued Jesus' family from Herod. Read Matthew 2:13-15 (page 734).

How did God warn Joseph?

THE LORD APPEARED TO JOSEPH IN A DREAM

How soon did they flee to Egypt?

IMMEDIATELY—THAT VERY NIGHT

The Passover Trip to Jerusalem

Now let's pick up the Luke narrative again. Read Luke 2:41-42 (pages 781-782).

This was a trip the family made every year at Passover, but this one was significant because of Jesus' age at the time. Jewish boys were initiated into the observance of Jewish ordinances when they were 12. They had been trained to fast, attend public worship, and learn a trade. From that time on they were considered sons of the law. It was an important milestone in any young boy's life.

And so it was in the case of Jesus. When the festival ended, the family, along with all their fellow travelers, headed for home. And shortly after that is when the excitement began. Read verses 43-45.

An ordinary day's journey varied from 18 to 30 miles, but on the first day of the journey the caravans would move slowly and stop after 8 or 10 miles (three hours). This way, if anything had been left behind, it would be possible for someone to return and get it in time to rejoin the caravan the next day.

Imagine Mary and Joseph's growing concern as they went from group to group looking for their son. Imagine when they realized He must still be in Jerusalem!

The several-hour walk back to Jerusalem to look for their son must have seemed endless. Mary's heart had to be pounding in dread and fear. Jerusalem was a large city. Where would they even begin looking?

One day passed—nothing! Another day passed. Can you imagine their anguish, their stark terror? And do you wonder if their anguish was even greater than other parents' would have been? This was no ordinary child they had lost—this was the Son of God!

And then at last they found Him. Read verses 46-47.
Where was Jesus?

IN THE TEMPLE

What was He doing?

SITTING AMONG THE TEACHERS (OF THE LAW) AND ASKING QUESTIONS

How did the people respond to Jesus' interaction with the teachers?

AMAZED THAT JESUS UNDERSTOOD SO MUCH AT HIS YOUNG AGE OF 12

Now read verses 48-49.

Oh, what a typical mother–child picture this paints—Mary's "How could you do this?" and Jesus' innocent "Do what?" It's a conversation every mother and child has had since time began, but there was a huge difference in this one. Jesus was doing what He had come to earth to do. He couldn't stop Himself from doing it. This wasn't Jesus, the son of Mary and Joseph, responding. This was Jesus, the Son of God, responding. And verse 50 shows the difficulty Mary and Joseph had with this.

What does it say?

THEY DIDN'T UNDERSTAND HIS REASONING

On a certain level, Mary and Joseph knew their son was unique— God had confirmed this to them over and over. But on a more ordinary level, an everyday-life level, this stretched the limits of their human comprehension. Oh, how many times they must have puzzled over what they saw and heard from Jesus as He grew up in their home!

Jesus knew His role that was given by His heavenly Father, but He also knew His role as a child of Mary and Joseph. Read verses 51 and 52. How did Jesus react to His parents?

HE WAS OBEDIENT TO THEM

Jesus waited about 18 more years before He began what is known as His public ministry. There was purpose in that space of time. And we can experience that same sense of God's purpose when we wait for His perfect timing. *(HE MATURED/GREW IN STATURE & FAVOR w/ GOD & MEN.)*

The Work of John the Baptist

Before we close this chapter, let's go back to Jesus' relative John. At 30 years of age John should have been serving in the Temple as a priest, like his father, Zechariah. But instead, he went into the wilderness in preparation for what God had called him to do—prepare the way for the coming Messiah. John was a very unusual man—a priest by birth, a prophet by the call of God, and a preacher who called people to repent and seek God's forgiveness.

Read about his ministry in Luke 3:1-6 (page 782).
According to verse 3, what did John tell the people that they should do?

repent of their sins

What did their baptism signify?

forgiveness for their repentance

Repentance from our sin is central to our personal relationship with God. How would you define sin?

sin is rebellion against God's will for us

Sin is any attitude, thought, or action that separates us from God. Sin is anything that we think or do that is in direct disobedience to what we learn and read in Scripture. And sin leads to unhealthy, debilitating actions.

Repentance is far more than just being sorry for our sin. Repentance is a move away from sin and toward God.

John explicitly told the people they needed to change the way they were living. He gave them specific instruction in how to change and that their new lifestyle should reflect their repentance. Read verses 7-14.

> John obviously wasn't interested in winning their affection, was he? How would you respond to someone who called you a snake?
>
> *probably defensively (in a personal confrontation) but more honestly in a "crowd".*

But there is a peculiar attraction to the truth. In spite of John's harsh tone, the people recognized he was speaking a truth that could change their lives. They didn't turn away from him. Instead they wanted more information.

> According to verse 8, how can you *"prove"* that you have turned from your sin?
>
> *produce appropriate fruit*

> What did John tell them to do regarding the poor?
>
> *share from your "abundance"*

> What did he tell the tax collectors and soldiers to do?
>
> *charge only what is due; don't take advantage*

He was very specific, wasn't he? Be generous to the poor, be honest in your business, don't lie, don't cheat, and be content with what you have. What is the common theme that runs through these specific instructions?

truth & fairness (righteousness)

They all require a turning away from self and turning toward the righteousness of God, don't they? They require repentance!

There is another very important point John makes to the people. Reread verse 8. What should it mean to them if they were descendants of Abraham?

no difference — all people are equal

Being descendants of Abraham did not automatically make them children of God any more than going to church makes us a Christian. John was calling the people to obedience to God—inwardly and outwardly—and that requires repentance. He wanted their attitude to change, knowing that would change their actions and then that would change their life.

According to verse 15, what were the people expecting, and who did they think John might be?

they were anticipating the Christ (their messiah)

How was John's ministry going to be different from the Messiah's ministry? Read verses 16-18.

John was baptizing with symbolic water baptism; the Christ would baptize with the Holy Spirit + fire (TRUE LIFE-CHANGING TRANSACTION).

John's message of repentance reached Herod Antipas (one of the sons of King Herod), who was the ruler of Galilee at the time, and it didn't set well with him. He didn't like being confronted with his sins. Read verses 19-20. What did Herod do to John?

had John put into prison

There's no doubt about it—speaking the truth can have consequences. But John courageously spoke the truth of God even though it landed him in prison. God needs courageous followers who are willing to speak the truth. Describe a time when you or someone you know suffered a consequence for speaking the truth.

We not only need to *speak* the truth, but we must also *live* the truth. People may argue with our words, but it is hard to argue with a life lived for God.

During Bill Clinton's presidency, Mother Teresa spoke passionately against abortion at the 1994 National Prayer Breakfast. At her conclusion, the audience leaped to its feet in a standing ovation. Later, during an interview, when asked about Mother Teresa's speech, President Clinton said, "How can anyone argue with a life so well-lived?"

That's the truth. Our life and our words matter. One without the other would limit us in reflecting the continuing work that Jesus Christ is doing in us and through us.

———————— *Personal Reflection and Application* ————————

From this chapter,

I see…

I believe…

I will…

❧

Prayer

Father, it is wonderful to know that when I confess my sins to you, you are faithful to forgive me my sins and cleanse me from all wickedness. Thank you for making it possible to go right into your presence with a sincere heart that fully trusts you. Thank you that my guilty conscience has been sprinkled with Christ's blood to make me clean (1 John 1:9, page 941, and Hebrews 10:22, page 926).

———————— *Thoughts, Notes, and Prayer Requests* ————————

_____

_____

3

The Preparation for Jesus' Ministry

One morning I heard my five-year-old son talking very earnestly to someone in his bedroom. Curious, I tiptoed down the hallway to see who it was. My son was sitting on his bed with our cat, Michael, in his lap. As he stroked Michael's fur, he explained how important it was to ask Jesus to forgive his sins. "Then Jesus will come live in your heart," he said.

I tiptoed back down the hall, smiling at my son's budding evangelism. I had second thoughts, however, when several minutes later he came up to me, with Michael still in his arms. "Mommy," he said, "our cat just became a Christian and now we need to baptize him!" The spirit of John the Baptist was alive and well in our son!

Prayer

Father, I know you saved me, not because of the righteous things I have done, but because of your mercy. You washed away my sins, giving me a new birth and new life through the Holy Spirit. Thank you for generously pouring out the Spirit upon me through Jesus Christ our Savior (Titus 3:5-6, page 918).

Jesus' Baptism

The first four books of the New Testament—Matthew, Mark, Luke, and John—are called the Gospels. None of them provide a complete biography of the life of Jesus. They include only the highlights of His time on earth. Since each writer had a different reason for writing his account, they each emphasized different things. One of the events they all refer to, however, is found in Luke 3:21-22 (pages 782-783).

Remember, John the Baptist told the people they were to be baptized to show they had repented of their sins. However, the Bible tells us Jesus was sinless. Read the following verses and note what they say about Jesus.

1 Peter 2:22 (page 935)

never sinned; was without deceit

1 John 3:5 (page 942)

no sin in Him

If Jesus was sinless, why do you think He was baptized?

He was our example; He taught baptism by example

Part of the answer is found in 2 Corinthians 5:21 (page 884). Who is the offering for our sin?

Jesus

Jesus did not become the offering for our sin until He was crucified, but His baptism was foreshadowing the time when He would take on our sins. At the Jordan River, Jesus identified Himself with us and our sin.

Another wonderful thing took place at Jesus' baptism. All three persons of the Trinity were clearly experienced by the people who were present.

- They saw God the *Son* be baptized.
- They saw God the *Holy Spirit* descend in the form of a dove.
- They heard God the *Father* speak from heaven, proclaiming Jesus as His dearly loved Son.

Wouldn't it have been amazing to actually be there? What would it have been like to hear God's voice coming from the heavens?

SHOCKING / UNBELIEVABLE / PUZZELING

Just as God proclaimed Jesus as His Son, so He proclaims us as His children when we commit our lives to Him. Read Romans 8:15-16 (page 862). What did you receive when God adopted you as His child?

SPIRIT OF SONSHIP —
FAMILY RELATIONSHIP w/GOD

According to verse 16, what is the evidence that we are children of God?

HOLY SPIRIT COMMUNICATES
THAT RELATIONSHIP WITH OUR SPIRIT

How incredible to feel God's Spirit affirming our spirit that we belong to Him—that we are His beloved children!

Luke is the only one who gives us the age of Jesus when He began His public ministry. Read Luke 3:23 (page 782). ("ABOUT 30")

Although Jesus was not a descendant of Aaron, this is also the age when priests began to serve in the Temple (Numbers 4:3, page 106).

Chapter 3:23-28 is the genealogy of Mary. Joseph's genealogy is given in Matthew. Matthew begins with Abraham and goes through David and his son Solomon, and all the way down to Joseph.

The genealogy in Luke is given in the reverse order. It begins with Mary's father and goes through David and David's son Nathan all the way back to Adam (1 Chronicles 3:5, page 309). Isn't it interesting that Luke, who wrote this book for the Gentiles and emphasized Jesus as the Son of Man, traced Mary's genealogy back to the first man, Adam?

The Temptation

In the first part of the Old Testament, we read about Eve and then Adam being tempted by Satan, referred to as the serpent. In the first part of the New Testament, just before Jesus began His ministry, we read about His being tempted by Satan, referred to as the devil. The two incidents make for an interesting comparison. Adam's temptation took place in a lush and magnificent garden where he had everything he could ever want. Jesus' temptation took place in a barren, empty desert.

Adam focused inward on himself and the one thing he didn't have in the midst of his abundance. As a result, he failed the test miserably. Jesus focused upward on His Father and all that came from Him. In spite of a severely weakened body (after 40 days without food), He was able to access the strength available to us through God. He was able to resist extreme temptation and experience victory. Let's look at the various ways Jesus was tempted.

Read Hebrews 4:15b (page 922). What type of temptations did Jesus have to endure?

of every type

What are some of the ways you find yourself being tempted?

Jesus completely, 100 percent understands your temptation. He has physically, emotionally, and spiritually been there—long before you were—and He knows how to help you!

Read Luke 4:1-2 (page 783). How long was Jesus in the desert being tempted? *(40 DAYS)*

Forty days! Do you know how weak and exhausted He must have been? And Satan, fully aware of His weakness, knew exactly how to tempt Him.

Read 1 Peter 5:8 (page 937). What does the devil *"prowl"* around looking for?

"Someone to devour"
(TO TOTALLY DISCREDIT/RUIN ONE'S REPUTATION OR CREDIBILITY)

Read 2 Corinthians 11:14 (page 887). What does Satan disguise himself as?

AN ANGEL OF LIGHT

(DESIREABLE, HELPFUL, UNDERSTANDING)

Let's look at the three ways Satan came at Jesus.

In Luke 4:3-4 (page 783), what physical desire did the devil first tempt Jesus with?

ABILITY TO CHANGE STONE TO BREAD

Right off the bat the devil hit Jesus with His most pressing need—food.

In Luke 4:5-8 (page 783), what did the devil tempt Him with?

POWER & AUTHORITY OVER "ALL THE KINGDOMS OF THE WORLD"

In Luke 4:9-13 (page 783), the third temptation, what did the devil try to get Jesus to do?

TO TEST GOD'S FAITHFULNESS TO HIM

Did you notice that with every temptation, Jesus had the same reply? What did Jesus always use to refute Satan?

GOD'S WORD ("IT IS WRITTEN")

The power in God's Word is immeasurable! It provides impenetrable protection. What does Psalm 119:11 (page 468) say?

with God's Word written on our hearts, we can avoid/resist sinning

The greatest protection against sin is knowing God's Word, having it readily accessible in your heart and mind. The third time the devil tried to use the Scriptures out of context to tempt Jesus. But he still failed, because Jesus knew the truth of the entire Scripture.

The best protection you can provide for yourself against any kind of temptation is to memorize Scripture. Even if you think you can't do it, try. It's planting divine concepts in your heart, and God will bring His Word to your mind just when you need it.

While it is very wise to be aware of Satan and his tactics, you do not need to live in fear of him. His power is nothing compared to God's power. God is all-powerful, in all, and through all; He is sovereign. Satan was defeated at the cross. Read the following verses.

1 John 4:4 (page 943)
Ponder this verse for a moment. Why have we already won the victory?

we have God (Jesus/Holy Spirit) in us — not to be separated

James 4:7 (page 932)
What does it say happens when you resist the devil's temptations?

the devil will flee from us

Don't you love that word? Flee! Not saunter, not mosey—Satan flat out flees!

Read 1 Corinthians 10:13 (page 876). This is such a great verse.

List the four clear points it makes.

1. _temptations are common to all people_

2.) _God is faithful_

3. _you won't be tempted beyond your ability to endure_

4. _God will provide a way out, so you may stand up under it_

Circle the one you find most encouraging.

It's hard to choose, isn't it? Each one is very powerful. God has put at our fingertips everything we could ever possibly need to be victorious over sin. He wants our success even more than we do.

When the Spirit of God led Jesus into the wilderness to be tempted by Satan, it wasn't to see if there were any flaws in Him, but rather to demonstrate that He was totally dependent on God and therefore did not sin. He wanted us to know we have a Savior who is holy, who has been tested in every way we are, and who fully understands our struggle, and still He remained sinless. That is why He is able to save us from our sin. Read Hebrews 7:25-26 (pages 923-924).

The People Don't Understand Jesus

As Jesus began to actively preach and teach, some people found it hard to accept what He said. Some of them remembered Him as a child. Some probably even remembered when He'd caused his parents such panic by staying behind in Jerusalem. Read Luke 4:14-22 (pages 783-784).

Imagine you have known Jesus all of His life and were in the synagogue when He came in and read from the sacred Scriptures. When He handed back the scroll, sat down, and announced, *"The Scripture you've just heard has been fulfilled this very day,"* what would your thoughts have been?

• that's pretty pretentious!
• does he mean himself or someone else he will reveal?

Do you think you might have struggled with the concept that the son of the carpenter was actually the Messiah you'd been waiting for all your life?

How did Jesus respond in verses 23 and 24?

he acknowledged their skepticism as "normal" and prophesied the "heal yourself" quote along with their inner thoughts

Read verses 25-27. They wanted Him to prove Himself to them by doing miracles like they'd heard He had done in Capernaum. Instead He gave them examples from the Old Testament of when Gentiles had been healed instead of Jews. (If you want, you can read about these miracles in 1 Kings 17:8-24, page 275, and 2 Kings 5:1-14, page 286.) He wanted them to accept Him as their Messiah by faith, not because of seeing a miracle.

How did the people react to this? Read verses 28-30.

they were furious + forced him out of town and onto a hill where they sought to throw him over and kill him

What do you think that angry mob did with their out-of-control emotions when, after dragging Jesus up to the top of the hill and over to the edge of the cliff, He simply passed through them? I wonder if they stared in amazement at their empty hands. Did they swipe the air, still trying to grab Him? Did anyone state the obvious—that they'd just witnessed a miracle of their own?

Traveling with Jesus

Jesus traveled widely during His ministry. He healed people and did other miracles in many places. Read the following passages and note what He did and how the people responded.

Luke 4:31-37 (page 784)

Jesus ordered a demon out of a "possessed" man in the synagogue — the people were puzzled at how Jesus could order evil spirits.

Luke 4:38-39 (page 784)

Jesus rebuked a fever & it left Simon's mother-in-law so that she was made well & able to wait on Jesus & Simon

Luke 4:40-44 (page 784)

Jesus healed all kinds of illnesses & cast out evil spirits — the people all tried to keep Him with them (but He went onto other cities to continue His mission)

Luke 5:1-11 (784-785)

After preaching from shore, Jesus had Simon take Him out on his boat so Jesus could preach more freely. Afterward He told Simon where to fish, and the catch was so abundant Simon had to get help. Simon recognized Jesus' power + miracle in this and became (along with the others: James + John sons of Zebedee) immediate disciples of Jesus.

(OBEDIENCE)

Luke 5:12-16 (page 785)

A leper begged Jesus for healing, which Jesus did. News of it spread rapidly & crowds of people sought Jesus for healings!

Luke 5:17-26 (page 785)

Jesus — before a crowd of onlookers, including Pharisees & teachers of the law — healed a paralytic man & forgave his sins. The official took issue with the "forgiveness", but crowd was amazed & praised God.

Luke 6:6-11 (page 786)

One Sabbath, in the synagogue, Jesus healed a man of his shriveled hand (knowing the Pharisees & teachers of the law were wanting to "catch" Jesus at "work" on the Sabbath). They

As you can see, the reactions to Jesus' miracles were varied. *began to plot against Jesus)*
Which reaction did you most identify with?

Amazed — awe-struck — praising God

After His temptation in the desert, Jesus jump-started His ministry by doing all of the healings and miracles we just read about. He was showing people the power of God. Now He needed a group of people who would follow and learn from Him during His ministry: His disciples.

Jesus Calls His Disciples

Let's go back to Luke 5:1-11, when Jesus called His first disciples. When Peter fell to his knees in awe of Jesus' holiness, Jesus said something that must have sounded peculiar to him at the time. Read verse 10. What did Jesus say they would now be catching?

they would be "catching" men

What do you think Peter thought when Jesus said that?

possibly a physical, hands-on "catching" of men in order to speak the gospel to them

But it's the next verse that is exquisite. How did Peter and his partners, James and John, respond in verse 11?

immediate, eager, "sold-out" commitment to follow Jesus

"*They left everything and followed Jesus.*" In spite of their questions, they wanted to go wherever He was going. It's how God longs for each of us to respond—wholly and without reservation.

What do you think it would look like in your life to leave everything and follow Christ?

Take time right now to tell God your heart's desire is to follow Him without reservation. Ask Him to help you. Leave behind all—attitudes, thoughts, things, and actions—that stands between you and Him.

Peter, James, and John were the first men Jesus called to be His disciples, or followers. Later, after He'd taught them all they needed to know, they became His apostles, or sent ones, commissioned to spread the Good News. He chose these men to be with Him, to spend time with Him and learn all they could. He wants us to be His disciples as well, learning all we can as we spend time in His Word and in prayer. He also wants us to be His "sent ones," or messengers, by revealing Him to the world through the way we live.

There were nine other men Jesus handpicked to be His disciples. Read Luke 5:27-32 (page 785) to learn about another disciple of Christ.

> Blue-collar fishermen and a despised tax collector. Jesus made interesting choices, didn't He? If you were putting together a group of people to whom you'd eventually entrust your life's work, are these the kind you would have sought out?
>
> *Doubtful*
>
> Luke 6:12-16 (page 786) gives a complete list of disciples Jesus chose to be apostles.
> *Simon (Peter), Andrew, James, John, Philip, Bartholomew, Matthew, Thomas, James (son of Alphaeus), Simon (the Zealot), Judas (son of James) & Judas Iscariot.*

Jesus did not choose perfect men. As far as the world was concerned, they were pretty insignificant. These men were representative of all humanity; He took them as they were and transformed them.

In verse 12, what did Jesus spend time doing before choosing
His disciples?

He spent the night praying to God

Jesus' communication with God was natural and continual. It
shows His total dependence, submission, and obedience to God's will.
It's exactly how God wants us to communicate with Him. He wants
us to depend on Him fully and trust to His guidance. The more time
we spend in communion with Him, the more accurately we will por-
tray Him to the world. Prayer produces calmness, courage, strength,
patience, and wisdom—all things we need for a well-lived life.

God wants us to communicate with Him, and He wants us to follow Him above everything else. Jesus chose 12 ordinary men to love
and teach and train to lead and serve. They may not have always had
the right answers or done the right things, but Jesus had a specific plan
for them. Jesus has a specific plan for you as well! He loves you and
died on the cross for you so that you can be reconciled to God and
bear spiritual fruit.

Take a moment and reflect on God's love for you. Feel free to
write out your thoughts.

Now, set aside all your insecurities and hesitations and write out
the specifics of how God has gifted you. What are your strengths
and abilities? If your mind is blank right now, just sit quietly for
a moment and ask God to bring these things to mind.

• *a general love for all types of people*
•

The list you just wrote (and you may want to add to it as you think further) is what you need to accomplish your purpose in this life. Thank God for these abilities. Ask Him to help you fully utilize them.

———— *Personal Reflection and Application* ————

From this chapter,

I see…

I believe…

I will…

————— ∽ —————

Prayer

Lord, from the first moment I followed you, I became your disciple. You have called me to share your Good News and make disciples of all the nations. I pray for strength and wisdom as I give up everything and follow you (Matthew 28:18-20, page 760, and Luke 14:33, page 797).

———— *Thoughts, Notes, and Prayer Requests* ————

_____

_____

_____

4

Jesus' Power Revealed

S he was the most evil woman I'd ever met!" The young woman was speaking about her mother-in-law, who'd caused much anguish in her marriage. "She lied about me to my husband and about my husband to me," she continued. "She interfered with our kids and pitted them against each other. If ever I had an enemy, it was her, and I didn't know what to do about God's command that we are to love our enemies."

She talked about one day when she was standing in front of a card rack, looking for a Mother's Day card for her own mom. *Buy one for her too.* The prompting came from deep within her spirit. *Buy one that describes the kind of woman you wish she was.*

"The very thought galled me," she said. "But I did what God prompted—and I kept doing it for every special occasion after that. One day I even sat down and wrote her a thank-you note for the great son she'd raised. The more cards and notes I sent, the easier it became and the less hypocritical it felt."

She described how the cards to her mother-in-law began to work a miracle. "The woman who'd been so cruel and mean began to soften—it was like she was trying to live up to the words on the cards I was sending her! Today, I can honestly say she is my friend, not my enemy."

It's just as God promised us! When we trust God and His ways, remarkable things happen because with God, nothing is impossible.

⬥

Prayer

Father, help me be the salt of the earth and the light of the world. Don't ever let my behavior become like a basket, hiding your light that is within me. Instead, let my life be like a lamp placed on a stand where it gives light to everyone. In the same way, let my good deeds shine out for all to see, so that everyone will see you and praise you (Matthew 5:13-16, page 736).

The Sermon on the Plain and the Sermon on the Mount

Throughout Jesus' ministry He repeated important teachings to many different groups of people and under different circumstances. The Sermon on the Mount, recorded in Matthew, and another sermon, referred to by some as the Sermon on the Plain, recorded in Luke, include some of the same topics, although the Sermon on the Mount is much longer.

The Sermon on the Plain goes from Luke 6:20-49. Let's first look at Luke 6:17-19 (page 786).

What different areas did the people come from?
ALL OVER JUDEA: FROM SEACOAST NORTH & WEST (TYRE & SIDON), AND INLAND TO JERUSALEM

Why did the people travel so far to see Jesus?
TO BE HEALED — TO TOUCH JESUS & RECEIVE THE POWER COMING FROM HIM

Now turn to Matthew 5:1 (page 735), where Jesus prepares to give a very similar sermon. What did Jesus climb up to preach this sermon?

ONTO A MOUNTAINSIDE

This is called the Sermon on the Mount, and it is much longer. It covers three entire chapters of Matthew, ending at Matthew 7:27 (page 738).

In the Sermon on the Plain, Jesus addressed four groups of people. Who are they? Read Luke 6:20-22 (page 786).

- *THE POOR*
- *THE HUNGRY*
- *THE SAD (THOSE WHO WEEP)*
- *THE PERSECUTED (BECAUSE OF JESUS / GOSPEL)*

In the Sermon on the Mount He defines these groups more thoroughly. Read Matthew 5:3 (page 736) and note who the "poor" are.

POOR IN SPIRIT

When we come to God, we recognize that we have nothing with which to gain His favor. According to Luke 6:20 (page 786), what do we gain from turning to God in our spiritual poverty?

WE GAIN THE KINGDOM OF GOD

Matthew 6:33 (page 738) says something very important about the Kingdom of God. What will happen when we seek the Kingdom above everything else?

ALL WE NEED WILL BE GIVEN TO US

We enter the Kingdom of God when we accept Jesus as our Savior. As part of God's Kingdom we have access to everything we need to live righteously.

The next group of people mentioned is the hungry. Read Matthew 5:6 (page 736). What do the hungry thirst for?

FOR RIGHTEOUSNESS

Justice is also translated *righteousness*. When you long for what is right and just, what will the result be?

THEY WILL BE FILLED

According to the last part of Luke 6:21 (page 786), what happens to those who are weeping?

THEY WILL LAUGH

I love the contrast of this verse! From weeping to laughing— a complete turnaround. That's what God does for us. Psalm 126:5-6 (page 473) paints a similar contrast. What is it?

sow in sadness; reap with joy

Think of a time when God turned your tears into laughter.

Luke 6:22-23 (page 786) paints another interesting contrast, a more challenging one because it involves controlling our attitude, which is never easy.

BE JOYFUL WHEN PERSECUTED BECAUSE OF STANDING FOR JESUS — REAP GREAT REWARDS IN HEAVEN

Did you feel blessed the last time you were hated or left out? When someone put you down for being a Christian, was your first thought, *Oh, wow! Think of all the blessings I'm going to get?* It's very difficult to have a good attitude in such times, but if we look beyond our circumstances and focus on God, our attitude will be transformed.

What does verse 23 say we should do?

REJOICE & LEAP FOR JOY

That is a picture of great joy, isn't it? I must remember to leap for joy next time. And it's possible to do that when we are focused on God and our future with Him rather than whatever mistreatment we endure now.

Jesus then issues some serious warnings. Read Luke 6:24-26. What is Jesus warning us against?

THOSE WHO ARE (ALREADY) WELL-OFF AND HAPPY IN THIS LIFE — WHO GET ALONG WELL WITH THE WORLD — CAN LOOK FORWARD TO JUDGEMENT HEREAFTER.

Jesus does not leave it at that. He goes into further detail of how we should act. He talks in-depth about loving our enemies. Read Luke 6:27-30 (page 786). What are the eight things Jesus tells us to do?

1. LOVE YOUR ENEMIES

2. DO GOOD TO THOSE WHO HATE YOU

3. BLESS THOSE WHO CURSE YOU

4. PRAY FOR THOSE WHO MISTREAT YOU

5. IF SOMEONE HITS YOU, DON'T RETALIATE (TURN YOUR OTHER CHEEK TO HIM)

6. IF SOMEONE STEALS YOUR CLOAK, ALSO LET HIM TAKE YOUR TUNIC

7. GIVE TO THOSE WHO ASK

8. IF SOMEONE TAKES FROM YOU,
   DON'T DEMAND IT BACK.

Ouch! Not a single one is easy, is it? How could you combine all eight into one summary statement?

Luke 6:31 (page 786) actually sums everything up perfectly. What does it say?

DO TO OTHERS AS YOU WANT THEM
TO DO TO YOU.

Transformed Living

In essence, Jesus is asking us to change our attitude, isn't He? He's telling us to stop reacting according to our natural instinct and react in a way that glorifies God. Is it impossible to do? On our own, yes. But God doesn't expect us to do it on our own. Read Romans 12:2 (page 866).

How does God transform us?

HE TRANSFORM OUR MINDS, RENEWING
IT TO DISCERN HIS GOOD & PERFECT WILL.

When our way of thinking changes, our behavior changes as well. Reacting in love and kindness becomes instinctive. The results of a transformed mind will be spectacular, not just personally, but with everyone you come in contact with. In fact, sometimes miracles happen, just as the young woman we read about at the beginning discovered with her mother-in-law.

Read Luke 6:32-36 (page 786). What characteristics of the Most High will help you achieve these lofty behaviors (verses 35-36)?

- *LOVE*
- *GOODNESS/KINDNESS*
- *GENEROSITY*
- *MERCY/GRACE*

Jesus' life was an example to us of one engaged in mercy and acts of compassion because of love.

When we align ourselves with God and commit to follow Him, He will always be calling us to a higher standard. Anybody can love people who love them back, but God wants us to be nice to people who hate us. That kind of behavior is not based on emotion, but on an act of the will. That's where transformation is demonstrated. The result is true transformation.

Jesus continues teaching about transformed living in the following verses. Read Luke 6:37-38 (page 786).

List the four attitudes or behaviors and each result.

1. *LOVE (NOT JUDGEMENT) — WON'T BE JUDGED*

2. *GRACE (NOT CONDEMNATION) — WON'T BE CONDEMNED*

3. FORGIVENESS ___ BE FORGIVEN

(faint pencil: EXPECTING)

4. GENEROSITY — RECEIVE IN GOOD MEASURE *(faint: ...)*

"Your gift will return to you in full." God will richly bless you for these attitudes and actions!

Read Luke 6:39-45 (page 787). What is the significance of removing the log from your eye before taking out the speck in your friend's eye?

BE HUMBLE & RECOGNIZE WE (NO ONE) KNOWS OR UNDERSTANDS EVERYTHING. WE MUST ALLOW GOD (THE HOLY SPIRIT) TO MINISTER "HIGHER" TRUTHS TO OTHERS IN THEIR TIME.

What does Jesus call us if we are not first removing our own log (verse 42)?

HYPOCRITES

Who is a fully trained student like according to verse 40?

LIKE HIS TEACHER

Jesus wants us to be like Him. As we become more like Jesus, our hearts will produce good fruit, because of Christ's working through us. Without Christ, our hearts are deceived.

The last four verses of this chapter draw a very important analogy for us to reflect on. Read Luke 6:46-49 (page 787).

Have you ever had someone ask for advice, only to have them do exactly the opposite of what you advised them to do?

YES!

Take care. We should be concerned if we simply go through the motions of reading our Bibles, joining Bible studies, even praying, if we are not going to follow Jesus' teachings. All those good things will have little benefit to us unless our lives are transformed. And without the power of God in us, holding us firm, we will fall.

The Concerns of John the Baptist

In the seventh chapter of Luke, we run into John the Baptist again, and a very interesting conversation takes place. Read Luke 7:18-20 (page 787).

What surprises you about this conversation?

WE EARLIER UNDERSTOOD THAT JOHN-THE-BAPTIST RECOGNIZED AND KNEW JESUS AS THE MESSIAH!

Now read John 1:32-34 (page 809). What does John testify about Jesus?

JOHN SAW THE "SIGN" OF THE DOVE (HOLY SPIRIT) COME DOWN & REMAIN ON JESUS — TESTIFIED THAT JESUS IS THE SON OF GOD.

In spite of everything he'd seen and experienced, John sometimes questioned things! Even as he continued to do what God called him to do—which was prepare the way for Jesus—he had doubts.

God, our Creator, understands our weaknesses that sometimes prompt such questions. He knows if they are honest questions based on a desire to understand Him better.

Turn to Luke 7:21-23 (page 787).

Jesus did not condemn John's questions. Instead, He answered them in two ways. First, He demonstrated His Godhood by performing several different miracles. Second, Jesus told John's disciples to go back and tell John what they had seen and heard. He fulfilled prophecy, knowing that John would recognize it (Isaiah 35:5-6, page 543). And it's the same today. We can find answers within the pages of our Bible. Just like John, don't be afraid to share your doubts with God and ask Him to lead you to the answers.

The Forgiven Woman

Further on in this chapter, we come to another interesting event. Jesus has been invited to dinner at the home of a Pharisee. Pharisees were a prominent sect of Jews who were more concerned with keeping traditional laws than God's laws. Jesus' teaching both confounded them and made them angry, because it offended their self-righteous attitude. Dinners such as these were sort of a public affair. Neighbors could come in and stand or sit around the wall and watch while the guests half reclined on couches while eating. As a guest, Jesus was reclining on a couch, possibly leaning on His arm as He dined and talked to His host.

Read Luke 7:36-38 (page 788). How was the woman described?

A WOMAN WHO HAD LIVED IN SIN —— NOW: HUMBLED & WEEPING (DEMONSTRATING A REPENTIVE HEART).

Why did the woman go to the Pharisee's house?

To ANNOINT (SHOW RESPECT FOR) JESUS — TO BLESS HIM

What did she do with the jar filled with perfume?

POURED IT ON HIS FEET

How much courage do you think it took for this woman, obviously known by all present to be immoral, to walk into the house of a Pharisee and approach Jesus?

TOTAL — AN ABANDONMENT OF HER OWN PERSONAL "SELF-WORTH"

Her attitude, though, is exactly the attitude that pleases God. Her focus was on Jesus, not on herself or what others would think of her. The picture of her unselfconscious humility is very moving, as her tears of repentance fall on Jesus' feet.

Read verses 39 and 40.

Don't you love it? Right in the middle of the Pharisee's self-righteous, judgmental thoughts, which he assumes are private, Jesus interrupts him. Jesus often spoke in parables as a reply to a question, request, or remark. He used these simple stories to illustrate a moral or spiritual lesson. However, this parable was given in answer to a *thought*!

Read verses 41-50.
Who represents the woman in this parable?

THE MAN WITH THE GREATER DEBT

Why did Jesus say that the woman's sins were forgiven (verses 48,50)?

JESUS RECOGNIZED HER FAITH (AND HER HUMBLE ATTITUDE OF REPENTANCE!)

How gently but succinctly Jesus put the Pharisee in his place. And how lovingly He forgave the woman! Who do you think slept better that night—the forgiven woman or the Pharisee?

A Look at Two Parables

The first parable is called the "Parable of the Farmer Scattering Seed" (or traditionally, "The Parable of the Sower"). Read Luke 8:1-8 (page 788).

What are the four different *"soils"* that the seed fell on?

1. *TRAMPLED-DOWN PATH*
2. *ROCK*
3. *AMONG THORNS*
4. *GOOD SOIL*

How many soils yielded a crop?

ONE

What do you think Jesus is illustrating in this story?

WE MUST EARNESTLY RECEIVE GOD'S WORD, "NOURISH" IT (STUDY) AND "PRODUCE" A "CROP" (FRUITFULLY SHARE THE WORD WITH OTHERS)

Now read verses 9-15 in the same chapter to see how Jesus explains the meaning.

The seed is God's Word. The people are the soil.
What did Jesus say about the seeds that fell:

on the footpath?

> THEY HEAR GOD'S WORD, BUT
> SATAN INTERFERES BEFORE THEY CAN
> BELIEVE & BE SAVED

on the rocky soil?

> THEY HAPPILY RECEIVE GOD'S
> WORD, BUT HAVE NO ROOT AND
> FALL AWAY IN TIME OF TESTING

among the thorns?

> THEY HEAR GOD'S WORD, BUT
> ARE OVERWHELMED BY THE WORLD'S
> WORRIES & DISTRACTIONS.

on the good soil?

> THEY HAVE GOOD, NOBLE HEARTS
> RECEPTIVE & RESPONSIVE TO GOD'S
> WORD; THEY HEAR, RETAIN & PERSEVERE
> (BEAR FRUIT).

Take a moment to reflect on these words of Jesus. Which kind of soil does your life resemble now? Ask God to help you to receive all of His Word and cause it to grow in you, so that your life reflects Him.

Now let's look at the Parable of the Lamp in Luke 8:16-18 (page 789).

Where should a lamp be placed and why?

> SHOULD BE UP ON A STAND, SO
> ITS LIGHT MAY BE SEEN &
> EXPERIENCED.

What will happen to those who listen to Jesus' teachings?

THE MORE THEY RECEIVE, THE MORE THEY WILL BE GIVEN

Read verses 19-21. At first you might think Jesus is being rude to His own family, but let's look at this in the context of the previous two parables. In both of these, Jesus focuses on those who are actively doing something toward their spiritual growth. In the first parable, Jesus said that those in whom God's Word finds good soil produce a harvest with it. In the second parable, Jesus says that those who actively listen and obey His teaching will receive understanding. In verses 19-21, Jesus shows the necessity and priority of hearing God's Word and obeying it.

Five Miracles of Jesus

Everywhere He went, Jesus performed a wide variety of miracles. Some people who witnessed a miracle became believers; others became afraid, and some even got angry. The reactions were as varied as the miracles. The eighth and ninth chapters of Luke (pages 789-790) tell about five different miracles Jesus performed. As you read about each miracle, fill out the chart on the following two pages, and then we'll see what we can learn from them.

Five Miracles of Jesus

The Miracle:	The Calming of the Storm	The Healing of the Demon-Possessed Man	The Healing of the Sick Woman	The Raising of the Dead Daughter	The Feeding of the Hungry Crowd
Scripture:	Luke 8:22-25	Luke 8:26-39	Luke 8:43-48	Luke 8:40-56	Luke 9:10-17
Who was the audience?	JESUS' DISCIPLES	• DEMON-POSSESSED MAN • TENDERS OF FLOCK OF PIGS • THE DEMONS	DISCIPLES, A CROWD & WOMAN WITH ISSUE OF BLOOD	JAIRUS & WIFE PETER, JOHN & JAMES	12 APOSTLES
What was the miracle?	JESUS CALMED THE RAGING SEA ("CONTROLLED NATURE")	JESUS CAST OUT A LEGION OF DEMONS FROM POSSESSED MAN	WOMAN TOUCHED JESUS' CLOAK & WAS INSTANTLY HEALED FROM LONG-TIME ISSUE OF BLOOD	12-YR-OLD GIRL RAISED FROM DEAD	JESUS FED ABOUT 5,000 PEOPLE BY BLESSING 4 LOAVES & 2 FISH
How was faith shown?	LACKING	MAN CRIED OUT TO JESUS, RECOGNIZING HIS DIVINITY	SECRETLY, TO BEGIN; THEN FEARFULLY ADMITTING HER PART IN RECEIVING POWER FROM HIM	EARLIER, THE FATHER TRUSTED JESUS WORDS OF ASSURANCE & CONTINUED TO HIS HOME	THE DISCIPLES OBEDIENTLY FOLLOWED JESUS' INSTRUCTIONS

	WIND & RAGING WATERS	LEGION OF DEMONS	ILLNESS; PHYSICAL INFIRMITY	DEATH	NATURE
What did God overpower?					
How did individuals or the crowd respond?	FEARFULLY	• MAN DESIRED TO GO WITH JESUS — BUT OBEDIENTLY SPREAD THE NEWS OF HIS HEALING; • MERCHANTS (OF PIGS) + OTHERS WERE FEARFUL & BEGGED JESUS TO LEAVE.	• WOMAN FEARFULLY BUT HONESTLY ADMITTED • DISCIPLES QUESTIONED JESUS' SENSITIVITY	CROWD LAUGHED AT JESUS' WORDS	THE CROWD ATE & WERE SATISFIED DOUBTLESS THE DISCIPLES WERE SURPRISED TO GATHER LEFTOVER FOOD!
What can I learn from this?	WE ARE SAFE IN JESUS' HANDS	THERE CAN BE MANY PERSPECTIVES & SELFISH RESPONSES TO THE SAME MIRACLE	JESUS KNOWS WHEN WE CALL UPON HIM	JESUS CAN BE TRUSTED AT HIS WORD, AND HE IS ALL-POWERFUL	JESUS UNDERSTANDS OUR NEEDS AND IS ABLE TO SUPPLY/FILL THOSE NEEDS

Look at what you wrote in the last row. Is there anything you cannot trust God to do in your life? Are you in the middle of a storm? Cry out for His intervention. Are you tormented by a person or circumstance? Cry out for God to calm your mind. Remember what we learned earlier—the more you cling to God's Word, the more clearly you will hear His voice.

Sending Out the Disciples

Jesus spent a year teaching and building up His disciples. When He felt they were ready, He sent them out. Mark 6:7 (page 766) says He sent them out in pairs. Read Luke 9:1-6 (page 790).

How did Jesus equip them?

(HIS) POWER & AUTHORITY TO DRIVE OUT DEMONS & TO HEAL DISEASES

What were His instructions to them?

DON'T TAKE ANY MONEY OR OTHER MATERIAL PROVISIONS — DEPEND ON HOSPITALITY OF HOSTS — IF NOT WELCOMED SHAKE DUST FROM FEET & GO ELSEWHERE

Why do you think Jesus told them to take nothing with them?

THEY SHOULD RELY UPON GOD'S PROVISION THROUGH WILLING SPIRITS OF "HOSTS" WHO WERE WILLINGLY SEEKING GOD'S TRUTH. — GOD WILL SUPPLY THEIR NEEDS —

The disciples were novices at spreading the news of the Kingdom. Until now they'd only followed Jesus and observed. Do you think perhaps Jesus wanted them to immediately experience the truth of Matthew 6:33 (page 738)?

How do you think the disciples felt as they headed out on their
own for the first time? Were they excited, nervous, scared—all
of the above? How would you have felt?

*ALL OF THE ABOVE. EMBARKING ON
A NEW ADVENTURE, BUT PROBABLY
ALREADY HUNGRY WONDERING WHERE THEIR
NEXT MEAL MIGHT COME FROM (AND WHEN ☺)*

It was one thing when Jesus was performing miracles, but when He
empowered others to perform miracles as well, His fame exploded. Even
Herod got word of what was happening. Read Luke 9:7-9 (page 790).

Why was Herod confused?

*RUMORS MISREPRESENTED THE
TRUTH — ALSO, HE HAD JOHN (BAPTIST)
BEHEADED & PROBABLY FEARED RETRIBUTION
IF JOHN HAD BEEN RESTORED TO LIFE!*

Now isn't that amazing? What did we just learn from the Parable
of the Lamp? That "*even what they think they understand will be
taken away from them.*" No wonder Herod was confused! He was
listening to other people instead of to Jesus!

But the disciples were clinging to everything Jesus said. They
were hungry to learn from Him and follow in His footsteps.
Read Luke 9:18-19 (page 790).

What question did Jesus ask them?

*HE WONDERED WHO PEOPLE
THOUGHT HE WAS*

How did they answer? *SOME SAID JOHN-THE-BAPTIST, OTHERS, ELIJAH OR AN ANCIENT PROPHET*

PETER ANSWERED CORRECTLY:

"(YOU ARE) THE CHRIST/MESSIAH OF GOD"

Their reply revealed much confusion among the public, but when Jesus put them on the spot, how did Peter answer, according to verse 20?

Do you ever feel confused about Jesus, about what you believe? What are some questions you ask yourself?

- *NOT ANY MORE*
- *BEFORE I WAS SAVED I DIDN'T RECOGNIZE JESUS' DEITY OR POSITION AS SAVIOR & CREATOR*

You can find answers everywhere, but the only answers you can depend on are the answers found in God's Word. *AMEN!*

Our Decision

Peter recognized Jesus as the Messiah sent from God. And we must recognize Him as our Savior as well, in order to have eternal life. When we make the decision to believe in Christ, we are making a decision that will permeate our entire life. Indeed, salvation is not a one-time event, never to be thought of again. Following Christ transforms your life and your living!

Have you made the decision to believe in and follow Jesus as Lord and Savior of your life?

YES!

If you are still uncertain about this, be encouraged that God wants to hear from you. You can let Him know your questions and doubts. He has answers for you. His peace can be yours. No matter what you have done, no matter where you have been, God wants you to know and believe that He loves you and wants to be in relationship with you. Jesus died for your sins so that you might be reconciled to—reconnected with—God. You can accept that free gift of salvation and start living out your faith. (For more information on how to become a Christian, you can read the "Know God" section near the end of this book on pages 185–187.)

Even now God is pouring His strength into you, enabling you to set your mind to seek Him above all else.

You will be amazed at how God will help you.

Personal Reflection and Application

From this chapter,

I see…

I believe…

I will…

Prayer

Father, as Peter confessed, Jesus is the Messiah sent from God. Please help me to hear Jesus' teachings, cling to them, and to put them into practice so that I may bear a fruitful harvest for you (Luke 9:20, page 790, and Luke 8:15, page 789).

Thoughts, Notes, and Prayer Requests

5

Jesus' Teaching

It had been a long, trying day of clashing wills with my five-year-old. Landon had spent the entire day pushing limits and testing boundaries. Bedtime came as a welcome relief to both of us. As I pulled back the covers of my bed, I found a note on my pillow. It was from my son, spelled phonetically as only a five-year-old can do.

> Dear mome
> I luv you. Im sory I wuz bad. From now
> on I will tri my best to be god.
> Sine, Landon

I smiled at his unwitting mistake in the final line. I knew he meant to say "good," but it gave me pause, nonetheless. Perhaps my standards were a bit too high for a five-year-old. Perhaps understanding on my part was as important as obedience on his part.

I thought about Jesus as He walked this earth, teaching His disciples and others. As high as His standards were that He held before them—even greater was His compassion and understanding when they stumbled. I went to sleep determined to make tomorrow a better day for both my son and me. With God guiding me, I would.

Prayer

Father, you care for wildflowers that are here today and thrown into the fire tomorrow, so I know you will certainly care for me. Forgive my little faith! Help me not to worry about what I'll eat or drink or wear. I realize these things dominate the thoughts of unbelievers, but they shouldn't dominate my thoughts, because you already know all my needs. You have promised that if I will seek you above all else, and live righteously, you will give me everything I need (Matthew 6:30-33, page 738).

Jesus Talks About the Cross

After Jesus asked the disciples who they thought He was and Peter proclaimed Him to be the Messiah, Jesus finally began to talk to them about His ultimate purpose, which was looming in the near future. Read Luke 9:21-22 (page 790).

Jesus gave them a lot of heavy information in just a few sentences, didn't He? Not the least of it was the *"raised from the dead"* part? What do you think their reaction to this information might have been?

IT PROBABLY FLEW OVER THEIR HEADS AS THEY TRIED TO CATCH ALL THE OTHER DETAILS HE SPOKE OF

But Jesus had even more to tell them—this news hitting even closer to home. Read Luke 9:23-27 (pages 790-791). What did Jesus say they had to do if they wanted to follow Him?

DIE TO SELF — BE TOTALLY "SOLD OUT" TO GOD & THE GOSPEL

This is the first time the cross is mentioned in Luke. The cross was known as an instrument of death, and Jesus was preparing them for what lay ahead and what the cost would be to them personally. When Jesus said that they were to take up their cross daily, He meant that they must daily make the commitment to deny selfish desires and to follow wherever He might lead them. There might be fear, rejection, or even physical death—those are some costs of discipleship. Following Christ comes with a cost—a cost we can't compare to the cost He paid in death on a cross—but a cost nonetheless. Jesus said when we lose our lives—our comforts, desires, ambitions (this list can go on forever), we will find them in Him.

More miracles followed after that, and everyone was in awe as Jesus continued to prepare the disciples for what was coming. Read Luke 9:43-48 (page 791).

Why didn't the disciples understand what Jesus said?

IT WAS VEILED/HIDDEN FROM THEM (BY GOD)

Why do you think they were afraid to ask Jesus for clarification?

THE PROBABLY DIDN'T WANT TO ADMIT THEIR "IGNORANCE" (LIKE: WHEN YOU DON'T UNDERSTAND A JOKE BUT LAUGH AS IF YOU DO ☺)

What did Jesus do when the disciples started to argue about who was the greatest?

GATHERED A NEARBY CHILD TO HIM AND USED THE "LESSER-IS-GREATER" EXPLAINATION.

How is the end of verse 48 related to the beginning of the Sermon on the Plain in Luke 6:20-23?

THE LOWLY IN LUKE 6:20-23 (THE PERSECUTED ONES) WERE ACTUALLY THE GREATEST IN GOD'S EYES. LIKEWISE, IN LUKE 9:48 THE "LOWLY" CHILD REPRESENTS SOMEONE "LESSER" THAN A "WISE ADULT" BUT IS ACTUALLY GREATER IN HIS DEPENDANCE (on God)

Our minds need to be transformed to think like Jesus thinks: The least will be the greatest. The poor will become rich in the Kingdom. The hungry will be filled. Those who weep will laugh, and the persecuted will rejoice. Oh, how contrary are our immediate thoughts to Christ's thoughts!

Opposition from the Samaritans

The time had come for Jesus to close the miraculous and healing part of His ministry. He now set His face toward Jerusalem, to accomplish His ultimate mission on earth—to die for our sins, so that everyone who believes might be saved by accepting His death in their place. On His way there, He ran into opposition. Read Luke 9:51-56 (page 791).

What was James and John's reaction to the Samaritans' rebuff?

THEY SOUGHT TO BRING DESTRUCTION UPON THE SAMARITANS.

How did Jesus respond to this great prejudice between the Jews and Samaritans?

JESUS REBUKED THEM AND PASSED ON TO ANOTHER VILLAGE

Think of what the Samaritans missed out on because of their prejudice. They missed a chance to personally meet the Messiah and experience transformation. Their closed minds closed the door to opportunity, just as our closed minds do.

In the final verses of this chapter we read about three different people who considered becoming a follower of Jesus. Read Luke 9:57-62 (page 791). What do you think Jesus is teaching about discipleship?

COMMITTED DISCIPLESHIP REQUIRES SETTING ASIDE WORLDLY CARES AND REMAINING CLOSE WITH GOD & HIS WORD ——— DON'T ALLOW WORLDLY MATTERS TO DISTRACT YOU FROM "KINGDOM-THINKING",

Did you notice the last verse? *"Anyone who puts a hand to the plow and then looks back is not fit for the Kingdom of God."* It is a strong statement, but there is a cost of discipleship that is expected when following Christ. The Christian life is not meant to be easy and comfortable. In all three of these encounters with Jesus, the priority of the person is not to follow Christ. Honoring your parents and family members is important, but it should never be an excuse or take priority over following Christ.

Jesus Sends Out Another Group of Disciples

The tenth chapter of Luke opens with Jesus sending out a large group of His disciples in the same manner and with the same instructions that He sent the 12 disciples out in chapter 9.

Read the following verses. Why did Jesus send the disciples out in pairs?

Matthew 18:19-20 (page 749)

2 OR MORE WHO AGREE TOGETHER IN PRAYER WILL RECEIVE ANSWERS TO THEIR PRAYERS — JESUS WILL BE THERE AMONG THEM.

Romans 15:2 (pages 867-868)

BUILD UP / ENCOURAGE ONE ANOTHER

Galatians 6:2 (page 894)

SHARE ONE ANOTHER'S BURDENS

Ecclesiastes 4:9-12 (page 507)

HELP FOR ONE ANOTHER — STRONGER TOGETHER AGAINST COMMON FOES — BEST WHEN BOUND TOGETHER IN CHRIST (3RD CORD)

I love Ecclesiastes 4:9 (page 507) that says, "*Two people are better off than one, for they can help each other succeed.*" It is much easier to feel like a failure or to grow discouraged if you are by yourself. A close friend who shares your commitment to God is a tremendous help in maintaining that commitment. How have you experienced God strengthen you through a friend?

✓

Read Luke 10:1-16 (page 792).

What did Jesus tell the disciples to do in Luke 10:1-2?

PRAY FOR (MORE) WORKERS TO HARVEST THE FIELD"

Why do you think this prayer is significant?

1. CONVICTED THEM TO GET BUSY
2. THEIR OBEDIENCE WOULD MOVE GOD / HOLY SPIRIT TO RESPOND

What is the main point of Jesus' instruction to the disciples?

THE MORE "FRUITFUL" THEY WERE IN GAINING NEW DISCIPLES (FOR THE LORD), THE MORE "WORKERS" THERE WOULD BE

LUKE 10:

Now read verse 17.

What two things show that the disciples were successful?

THE "72" RETURNED, JOYFULLY REPORTING TO JESUS THEIR SUCCESS IN COMMANDING DEMONS (MIRACLES)

Read verses 18-24. *(LUKE 10:18-24)*

According to verses 18-20, how did Jesus respond?

THEY SHOULD REJOICE IN THEIR SALVATION & NOT IN THE MIRACLE POWERS JESUS GAVE THEM

Why did Jesus rejoice in the Holy Spirit?

JESUS REJOICED THAT THESE TRUTHS WERE REVEALED TO THE "SIMPLE"/PLAIN PEOPLE WHO FOLLOWED HIM, AND NOT TO THE SELF-IMPORTANT & SO-CALLED "WISE" OF THE WORLD.

God had revealed these blessings to the disciples, "*the childlike,*" when they have been hidden from the wise and clever. These men were willing to put Jesus' purposes and other people ahead of their own self-ish motives. They succeeded in taking up their cross. Jesus gave these men authority to overcome much of the enemy's power. The disciples' success revealed Jesus' power over Satan. Whenever the power of evil tempts us, we need to claim the protection of the Lord Jesus Christ as our Deliverer.

Jesus' response to the disciples in verse 20 was extremely impor-tant—and it's still important to us. The disciples were flush with success. They were feeling powerful and invincible—and indeed, because of God they were. But Jesus told them not to rejoice in that. Instead, what did He tell them to rejoice about?

THEIR SALVATION (NAMES IN HEAVEN)

When it's all said and done, nothing matters but that our name is written down in heaven. Nothing matters but our salvation gained through Jesus' death and resurrection. Let's stop right here and rejoice in that very fact.

AMEN ! ♡

More Parables

Each of the Gospel writers majored on a different aspect of the life, works, and teachings of Jesus. For example, Mark wrote about many more of Jesus' miracles. Dr. Luke, on the other hand, wrote about many more of Jesus' parables. Let's look at one of the best-known parables. Even people unfamiliar with the Bible are familiar with this one. Organizations have taken their name from this parable; philosophies have been built around it. It's even a term in the dictionary. Can you guess which parable it is?

The parable came about as the result of a question asked by a man who was a religious expert. His intent was to test Jesus. He wanted to see how He would answer. The question was, *"What should I do to inherit eternal life?"* As Jesus often did, He answered by asking another question. He asked him what the Law of Moses said about it. Read Luke 10:25-28 (page 792), and note the man's answer.

DO THIS (LOVE GOD WITH ALL YOUR HEART & SOUL / LOVE NEIGHBOR AS SELF) AND YOU WILL LIVE.

Jesus told him he was right, but the man, trying to justify his actions, side-stepped the heart of the issue he himself had brought up and asked another question: *"And who is my neighbor?"* (verse 29). And that is when Jesus told the Parable of the Good Samaritan.

Let's read the full parable first, and then we'll go back and look at it more closely. There are so many rich aspects to this story! Read Luke 10:30-37 (page 792).

To set the scene for where this story unfolds, picture the following: The road from Jerusalem to Jericho descended more than 3000 feet in less than 15 miles as it wound through gorges that were infested by robbers. This was not a safe road to be on by any stretch of the imagination. Yet many priests and Levites who lived in Jericho frequently passed that way in order to get to Jerusalem.

Who was the first to bypass the wounded man (verse 31)?

LUKE 10:

A PRIEST

In the interest of full disclosure, it is important to know that according to Jewish law, if the priest had touched a dead man, he would have been considered unclean. He would not have been able to participate in his Temple privileges until he'd gone through the purification process. To have helped the man would have been a great inconvenience to him.

The second man to pass by was a Temple assistant. All the same laws applied to him, and he made the same choice. His example is more horrifying, though, because he went for a closer look at the situation. He saw how wounded the man was, the blood and bruises—and still did nothing. Both religious men chose ritual over relationship and convenience over compassion.

As outrageous as it seems, if we'll be honest with ourselves, we make the same choice as these two men in a hundred different ways. What are some excuses you've used for not lending a helping hand when the opportunity presented itself?

According to verse 33, who finally helped the man?

SAMARITAN MAN

Back up for just a minute. Do you remember earlier when Jesus was going to visit Samaria? What was the Samaritans' response to Jesus? What a wonderful picture this paints of Jesus' attitude! He'd been rejected by the Samaritans and yet now, in His parable, He makes a Samaritan the good guy!

Now read verses 34-35. Talk about going the second mile! The Samaritan did all that and more for this stranger he'd never met. The amount of money he gave the innkeeper was worth two full days' wages, so he was not only generous with the wounded man, but he was generous with the innkeeper. His attitude was like that of Jesus!

God had blessed the Samaritan with the money to take care of the wounded man. God also blesses us with abundant resources to use for His glory—we need to be willing to use them to be a blessing to others. His purpose for us is to glorify Him in every behavior, and He, in turn, will pour out blessings with enough left over to share (2 Corinthians 9:8, page 886).

The parable ends with a clear definition of who our neighbor is. Read verses 36 and 37. What do they say?

THE SAMARITAN (WHO DEMONSTRATED MERCY) WAS/SERVED AS THE WOUNDED MAN'S NEIGHBOR. (THE OTHERS WERE, BUT DIDN'T ACT LIKE IT!)

Who is our neighbor? Whoever is in need.

In a larger sense, the Parable of the Good Samaritan is a picture of what Jesus did for us. He, the ultimate Good Samaritan, found us, desperately wounded by sin, dying alongside the road of life. Religion couldn't rescue us; being a good person couldn't rescue us. But then Jesus came along, bound up our wounds, healed our sin, and set us on the path of eternal life. That's not a parable—that's reality!

Choosing the Better Thing

There was a brother and his two sisters whom Jesus loved deeply and visited often. Luke tells us about one particular visit that ended up providing a powerful example that's been used through the centuries. Each sister chose a different way of showing her love for Jesus. Read Luke 10:38-39 (page 793). What did each sister do?

> MARY — SAT & LISTENED TO JESUS
>
> MARTHA — RUSHED AROUND PREPARING & SERVING JESUS & GUESTS

What do you usually do when someone you love comes to visit you? How do you express your feelings for them?

> Sit & visit (over easy snacks)

In the beginning neither sister was wrong. Mary was giving Jesus her full attention and Martha was giving Jesus' needs her full attention. Both are important acts of love. But somewhere along the way, as she cared for Jesus' needs, Martha stopped focusing on Him and started focusing on Mary. What happens in verse 40?

> ASKED JESUS TO CHASTISE MARY & MAKE HER HELP (justifying her own "busyness" & drawing attention to her own extra efforts)

How did Jesus respond to her complaint in verses 41 and 42?

> Jesus basically told Martha to calm down and choose the better priority: spiritual teaching by Jesus. Also, He would not take from Mary what she had properly chosen.

Jesus did not praise sentiment at the expense of practical service. The lesson is, in His words, "*You are worried and upset over all these details.*" We need to be careful not to allow legitimate cares to hinder our fellowship with the Lord Jesus. Do you find yourself in conflict between these two aspects of life?

busy, back-and-forth mind — hard to focus sometimes

What are some things you can change that will help you find a better balance between doing and being?

X

The Importance of Prayer

Read Luke 11:1-4 (page 793).

Prayer was a vital part of Jesus' life. He modeled the need to keep close to the heart of God and be refreshed by His presence. At night and very early in the morning, He would slip away alone to pray. Luke especially emphasizes the prayer life of Jesus. He shows us how completely dependent Jesus was on God the Father. When you look at the prayers Luke recorded, you'll see that Jesus always referred to God as Father. He taught His disciples to do the same. Once, when they specifically asked Jesus to teach them to pray, He gave them an example to follow. It's known as the Lord's Prayer, and while the more familiar version is in Matthew 6:9-13 (page 737), Luke also includes it.

What are the three things we are to ask for, according to verses 2-4?

(honor/show respect to God/" hallowed" name)
1. GIVE US DAILY BREAD (provide our needs)
2. FORGIVE OUR SINS (as we show grace to others)
3. KEEP US FROM TEMPTATION

Jesus gave His disciples an illustration about how we should pray in Luke 11:5-12 (page 793).

Why will the friend get up to give you the bread (verse 8)?

because of persistence

Now read verses 9 and 10. What will happen when we ask, seek, and knock?

ask — receive answer
seek — find
knock — door (answer) will be opened

This is such an encouraging passage of Scripture, isn't it? God doesn't mind our persistence, in fact He encourages it. Don't stop praying!

What prayer have you been praying for a while that you haven't seen any answers from God yet?

X (couple, living together)

How many times have you thought about giving up on it?

Take a moment right now and thank God for what He is doing in this matter, even though you can't see it. Tell Him that you trust His timing, and then pray once again for whatever it is.

Jesus valued prayer! That's why the Bible is full of Scriptures telling us why we should pray. Look up the following verses and note what they say.

Matthew 26:41 (page 758)

- BE ALERT & BE IN PRAYER TO RESIST TEMPTATION.
- OUR SPIRIT HAS RIGHT DESIRES, BUT OUR BODIES ARE WEAK

James 1:5 (page 930)

ASK GOD FOR WISDOM & HE WILL GIVE IT

John 16:20-24 (page 825)

BELIEVERS' GRIEF IN THIS WORLD WILL BE TURNED TO JOY WHEN JESUS RETURNS. THIS WORLD GIVES MUCH PAIN, BUT THAT WILL BE FORGOTTEN IN THE LIGHT OF THE HEREAFTER.

1 Thessalonians 5:17 (page 907)

PRAY CONTINUALLY (INCLUDING PRAISE!).

Jesus' teaching began to draw tremendous crowds. Always mixed in among the crowds were Pharisees and religious leaders, who became outraged by His claim to be the Son of God. Jesus openly criticized their self-righteous behavior. *"You Pharisees are so careful to clean the outside of the cup and the dish,"* He told them, *"but inside you are filthy—full of greed and wickedness!"* (Luke 11:39, page 794).

He spoke only the truth, but they continually tried to trick Him into saying something worthy of arrest. Jesus steadfastly kept His mind focused on what He'd come to do. As His time grew shorter, He prayed more frequently. Prayer is what kept Him connected to God while He was living on earth in the limitations of a human body. Prayer is what keeps us connected to God. Through prayer our weakness becomes God's strength and, as we've already learned, with God nothing is impossible.

———— *Personal Reflection and Application* ————

From this chapter,

I see…

I believe…

I will…

———————————— ✑ ————————————

Prayer

Father, thank you that you are close to all who call on you, who call on you in truth. I know that you grant the desires of those who fear you and that you hear my cries for help and rescue me. Thank you for the assurance that you answer me before I even call to you. While I am still talking about my needs, you will go ahead and answer my prayers (Psalm 145:18-19, page 479, and Isaiah 65:24, page 568).

———— *Thoughts, Notes, and Prayer Requests* ————

10/26

6

Jesus Trains His Followers

My friend's seven-year-old daughter came running up to her in tears. "Mommy, Brad and Jennie won't let me play with them!"

My friend went to investigate, asking why her older children wouldn't let their sister play with them.

"But Mommy, we *are* letting her play," Jennie said. "We're playing school and she's absent today!"

It took some creative thinking on their part, but Jennie and Brad had found a legitimate way to exclude their little sister, who kept interfering with their game. They were behaving a bit like the Pharisees we'll be looking at today, whose exclusionary attitudes worked overtime in their attempt to prevent Jesus from teaching.

Prayer

   Father, I ask that I will no longer be immature like a child. Don't let me be tossed and blown about by every wind of new teaching. Keep me from being influenced when people try to trick me with lies so clever they sound like the truth. Instead, let me speak the truth in love, growing in every way more and more like your Son, Jesus (Ephesians 4:14-15, page 897).

Considering Our Motives

Chapter 12 of Luke (page 794) opens with Jesus speaking to a crowd of thousands. Read Luke 12:1-5. There were so many people they were stepping on each other! As Jesus spoke, He cautioned and taught them. He spoke about the motives that guide our conduct, and He warned that someday every secret thing will be known. This thought should give us pause, knowing that nothing is hidden from God!

He cautions the people to fear God (verse 5), meaning to have deep reverence for Him. Read Proverbs 9:10 (page 486). What is the fear of the Lord? *beginning of wisdom*

What does knowledge of God result in?

understanding

The more we know God, the more capable we will be in navigating the challenges of life in a healthy, productive way. This was a central thought of Jesus' teaching. Read the following verses, and note the point He was making.

Luke 12:6-7 (page 794)
Trust God — He cares for all Creatures and knows your needs — He will provide

Luke 12:15 (page 795)
A person's life is valued above all else — his worth isn't measured by his possessions

Luke 12:16-21 (page 795)

The "abundant life" should be measured spiritually, and not by material luxury (SPIRITUAL IS FOREVER—MATERIAL STAYS BEHIND).

Count the "I's" and "my's" in Luke 12:17-19. This is a perfect example of how self-involved we can become—more focused on our physical well-being than we are on our spiritual well-being. In what ways do you find this to be true in your own life?

(10 + 1 "you")

TYPICAL CHRISTIAN ATTITUDE IS, GOD WANTS US TO "PROSPER"— SO, WE SHOULD HAVE A NICE, BIG HOME, CAR, ETC. TO DEMONSTRATE GOD'S PROVISION IN OUR LIVES.

These things aren't wrong, some are good for us. The danger comes when we place a higher priority on them than on our commitment to God. Read Luke 12:22-31 (page 795).

What is life more than (verse 23)?

MORE THAN FOOD

Why do we not need to worry about our needs (verse 30)?

GOD KNOWS WHAT WE NEED

Read Luke 12:32-34 (page 795).
How can we find out where our heart's desires lie?

WHERE OUR "TREASURE" IS—— WHAT WE FOCUS ON AND PURSUE THE MOST.

Jesus taught frequently on the subject of generosity versus greed, because He knew this is where we often get hung up. The temptation to build up treasure in this life is relentless. But the more we focus in that direction, the less satisfaction we will feel.

Read Luke 12:35-48 (page 795). It is important to note that Jesus is talking to faithful servants and also to people claiming to be servants of His. This section of Scripture, while harsh in its tone, clarifies the commitment that is involved when we choose to follow and serve Christ.

Who will be rewarded when Jesus returns?

THE ONE WHO KNOWS AND DOES THE LORD'S WILL (THE OBEDIENT)

When will the Son of Man come?

WHEN NOT EXPECTED

What question did Peter ask Jesus?

WHETHER THE PARABLE WAS JUST FOR THE DESCIPLES — OR FOR EVERYONE.

How severe is the punishment for those who claim to be Christ's servants, but are not?

VERY — THEY WILL BE CAST OUT WITH "UNBELIEVERS"

What is the significance of verses 47-48?

GOD DEMANDS LESS FROM PEOPLE WHO DO NOT KNOW THE TRUTH.

Making Choices Because of Jesus

Read Luke 12:49-53 (page 795).

Jesus causes people to choose between good and evil, between light and darkness. As a Christian we must choose to be on Christ's side, and sadly, that will sometimes cause painful divisions that can be very difficult to live with. How have you experienced this in your life?

HARD to HAVE A HEART-FELT RELATIONSHIP WITH THOSE WHO DON'T BELIEVE —— THE IMPORTANT SPIRITUAL DIMENSION IS MISSING.

How do you respond to the division?

MOSTLY JUST AN INTERNAL EMPTINESS IN THE "RELATIONSHIP"

Read Luke 12:57-59 (page 796).

Ouch! Verse 57 kind of stings, doesn't it? *"Why can't you decide for yourselves what is right?"* The answer is usually fairly simple—because each party is more focused on themselves than on God. When your first concern is self, the issue will always be complicated. When your first concern is glorifying God, your perspective becomes much clearer.

Read Luke 13:1-5 (page 796).

The people assumed the victims Jesus spoke of were terrible sinners because of what happened to them, but Jesus said that was not true. All people are sinners. The whole nation was deserving of judgment if they did not repent. Jesus used these incidents to teach that such destruction is the future of anyone who does not come to God for salvation before it is too late.

Read Luke 13:6-9 (page 796).

During His earthly ministry, Jesus spent time teaching His listeners how to be fruitful. But this parable shows Jesus' immense mercy and grace toward His creation. For three years the fig tree had borne no fruit and the owner was ready to cut it down, but the gardener, who believed in its potential, wanted to work with it a little longer. Jesus knows our potential for bearing fruit, and He is willing to keep working with us to make that happen.

Read another passage in which Jesus taught about the fruit in our lives—John 15:1-16 (page 824).

God produces "fruit" in us as we stay in close relationship to Jesus. We only produce good fruit through and by Him. Some examples of good fruit that please God are: teaching spiritual truth to others, praise and thanksgiving, good works with proper motive, winning people to Christ, providing from love for those in need, and exhibiting all the characteristics of Christ in our own lives.

Read Luke 13:22-30 (page 796).
Jesus makes the choice very clear, doesn't He? And the consequences of making the wrong choice are terrible. Yet the Bible tells us that very few will make the right one. Why do you think so many who will try to enter God's Kingdom will fail?

ESPECIALLY TODAY, MANY THINK BECAUSE THE WALK THE CHURCH AISLE THAT THEY'RE "SAVED" — BUT, SALVATION REQUIRES MORE: REPENTENCE, OBEDIENCE, "COMMUNION" (COMMUNICATION) IN SPIRIT

Verse 24 says that *"many will try to enter but will fail."* What a heartbreaking verse this is, and so avoidable! Jesus left nothing unanswered about the way to eternal life. He made it so clear and simple. Read John 14:6 (page 823). Who is the way to eternal life?

> JESUS IS THE WAY
> TRUTH
> & LIFE.

And yet people keep trying to complicate it. They go to the wrong source for answers, or they devise "feel-good" answers of their own. But the choice is clear and the choice must be made.

The choice becomes difficult depending on where we fix our focus: self or God. A self-focus complicates the issues, raising all kinds of distracting questions and creating a gap between God and us that feels insurmountable. That's why Jesus chose to lay down His life for us—to make the way to God accessible. As we lock our eyes on God and set our minds to follow Him, He enables us to make the right choice—the choice that leads to eternal life and abundant life here and now!

The Heartbreaking Reactions of the Jews

This chapter draws to a close with a sad picture. Read Luke 13:31-34 (pages 796-797).

What does Jesus mean when He says that Jerusalem wouldn't let Him, like a hen, gather its children beneath His wings?

> THE LEADERS (PRIESTS & TEACHERS OF
> THE LAW) JEALOUSLY GUARDED THEIR OWN
> HIGH POSITIONS & POISONED PEOPLE'S MINDS AGAINST
> JESUS.

I once saw a poignant photograph that illustrates this. A chicken had burned to death in a fire, and the photo showed the moment a fireman bent over for a closer look. As he lifted up a charred wing, five baby chicks came scurrying out from beneath her dead body. The chicks had lived because she had died. That's the picture Jesus portrays here as He looks out over the city He loves, a city whose citizens will very soon condemn Him to a terrible death. His grief is because they refuse to be gathered under the wings of His protection. Jesus triumphed over death, but the people who reject Him will not.

Sometimes misinterpreting Old Testament laws distracted the Jews from God. Jesus persistently confronted them in regard to these laws, trying to nudge them toward something so much better. Read the following Scriptures and note the focal point of what Jesus was teaching. Then look up the verse in the second column to see how that teaching can be applied to your life.

Scripture	What was the focus of Jesus' teaching?	How can I apply this to my life?
Luke 14:1-6 (page 797)	JESUS HEALED ON THE SABBATH DAY DO GOOD ON THE SABBATH.	Matthew 12:12 (page 742)
Luke 14:7-11	DON'T PUT ON AIRS & REGARD SELF ABOVE OTHERS AND BE THOUGHTFUL OF OTHERS RESPECTFUL	Philippians 2:3 (page 900)
Luke 14:12-14	BE GRACIOUS TO OTHERS WHO ARE LOWLY & IN NEED (NOT EXPECTING A REWARD) MERCY LIVE GODLY WITH GRACE & TOWARD ALL	Romans 12:1-2 (page 866)
Luke 14:15-24	GOD INVITES US FOR SALVATION BUT IF YOU REJECT THE INVITATION YOU'LL BE REJECTED FROM SALVATION	Mark 16:15 (page 778)

PARTICIPATE IN THE "INVITATION"
PROCESS SO MORE WILL HAVE
THE CHANCE FOR SALVATION
(WE ARE GOD'S VOICE IN
THIS WORLD)

Being a Disciple of Jesus

Luke 14:25-35 (page 797) talks about the cost of discipleship; it shows what a disciple of Christ must be willing to do.

What must we do to be Christ's disciple?

GIVE UP EVERYTHING
(REMEMBER: EVERYTHING ALREADY BELONGS TO GOD!)

What must we do before we become a Christian/disciple?

COUNT THE COST — CONSIDER WHETHER YOU CAN "COMMIT".

As disciples, what are we supposed to be like (verses 34-35)?

SALT (SPICY / A "HEALING" / "PRESERVING" AGENT)

We have to count the cost of discipleship before we begin the journey.

What do you see to be some of the costs of following Jesus?

* *SET-ASIDE (DEDICATED) TIME IN HIS WORD*
* *SEPARATION FROM OLD "FAMILIAR" PLACES/HABITS*
* *POSSIBLE/PROBABLE "RIDICULE" FOR BEING "GOODY-GOODY" OR "JUDGEMENTAL"*

What does the overall portrait of a disciple as depicted in these verses look like?

ONE COMMITTED TO A WHOLESOME & DISCIPLINED LIFE, CARING FOR OTHERS AND HONORING TOWARD GOD.
"SET" TO DO RIGHT AND NOT BE "BULLIED" INTO THE WORLD'S BEHAVIORS.

It's one of complete surrender, isn't it? Again and again, Jesus calls us to surrender every aspect of our being to His higher calling, and it's always for our greater good. It calls for much love, perseverance, patience, and wisdom; but oh, it will be worth everything we surrender a thousand times over.

Remember, God doesn't ask anything of us that we cannot do. He is the God of the impossible, but He knows our limits. What does He say in Matthew 11:29-30 (page 742)?

WHEN WE ARE BOUND TO HIM (YOKED TOGETHER), HE HELPS MAKE THE WAY EASY.

How do these concepts of total surrender and an easy yoke not conflict with each other?

HE TAKES THE LEAD AND THE OVERALL BURDEN.

The more closely we walk with God, the greater our awareness of the work He is completing in us.

A disciple is a person completely dependent upon Christ—a person who, because of love for God, is committed to His ways, knowing He will enable her or him to follow those ways. True disciples devote themselves to carrying out His interests rather than their own. Their one aim is to please Him, and they faithfully follow His direction in accomplishing the work He has given them to do.

Take some time to reflect on our discussion of being a disciple of Jesus.

What attitudes do you need to change?

What habits do you need to let go of?

What habits do you need to develop?

Better use of time (and energy)

──────── *Personal Reflection and Application* ────────

From this chapter,

I see…

I believe…

I will…

Prayer

Lord, you set the example of what real love is when you gave up your life for me. So help me now to be willing to give up my life for my brothers and sisters. Help me always be generous with my time and money so that if I see someone in need, I will show compassion and thus exhibit your love within me. Don't let me merely say I love others; let me show the truth by my actions (1 John 3:16-18, page 942).

Thoughts, Notes, and Prayer Requests

7

Parables of Jesus

I t was late at night and we were driving home after a long, exhaust-
ing day in a city on the other side of our state. We were all tired
and still had another two hours of driving ahead of us. We were
also hungry. Our boys kept begging us to stop and get some food, but
my husband and I were out of cash. Besides, the cafes we passed were
all closed. Then, passing through a little mountain village, we saw a
sign on a lighted reader board proclaiming, "Shish-kabobs! $3/ea."

"Please stop! Please stop!" our boys cried in unison.

I looked at my husband. "Surely we can scrape together three dollars and share one." My husband pulled into the parking lot.

"Okay," he said, "the only way we can get a kabob is if we can come
up with three dollars. Boys, check your pockets and look under the
floor mats. Mom will check her purse, and I'll look around up here in
the front seat." Instantly we were on a mission to come up with three
dollars.

"I found a dime!" Tyler shouted.

"I found a nickel!" Landon chimed in.

While I emptied my purse, my husband emptied his pockets. In
no time at all we were at $2.85. "Keep looking," I urged. "There's got
to be fifteen more cents in this car." For several minutes there was the
sound of more frantic searching.

"Pray, everyone! Pray!" Tyler shouted, just as Steve found a dime in the ash tray. But then our luck ran out. No matter how hard we looked, we were still short a nickel. Our hungry disappointment was sharp indeed as we reluctantly admitted defeat.

Steve and the boys decided to use the restroom before moving on. He opened the car door, and the interior light picked up a glint of something on the ground at his feet. He bent over and picked up a nickel!

Talk about celebration! We all whooped and hollered. I remained in the car while the guys went in to purchase a single kabob. In no time at all they came dashing back to the car—their hands *full* of kabobs. The restaurant was closing and the owner was just going to throw the kabobs away, so he sold them all to us for our $3!

What a celebratory feast we had—with food to spare—as we drove home exulting in God, for whom nothing is impossible.

Prayer

Father, build in me the same attitude that Jesus had. Though He was God, He did not think of equality with God as something to cling to. Father, just as Jesus gave up all that was His, let me give up all of me in order to be used fully by you. Don't let me cling to anything or anyone so that when others look at me they see you (Philippians 2:5-6, page 900).

Perhaps you've noticed by now that Jesus didn't argue with the people who challenged His teaching. Instead, He responded with a story, and who can argue with a good story—and one that reflects the truth?

The Lost Sheep and the Lost Coin

Three of the parables we're going to look at can actually be grouped together as one, revealing God's grace and love for the lost. These parables are found in chapter 15 and are rich examples of God's love and His great rejoicing in salvation. The first story is the Parable of the Lost Sheep. Read Luke 15:1-7 (pages 797-798).

> Oh, what a wonderful picture this paints of God! What is the first thing the shepherd does when he discovers one sheep is missing? *HE LEAVES THE OTHERS TO GO SEARCH FOR THE MISSING ONE.*

Imagine! He leaves all the other sheep—99 to be precise, which seems like a lot of sheep to me—in the wilderness.

> At the end of this parable, we understand why the shepherd was willing to leave the other sheep in the wilderness. How did Jesus describe the 99 others in verse 7?
> *THEY ARE RIGHTEOUS & DON'T NEED TO REPENT.*

They were well-taught sheep who were trustworthy. He could count on them to stay put in his absence.

> How long does the shepherd look for his lost sheep?
> *UNTIL HE FINDS IT (AS LONG AS IT TAKES!)*

There's no time limit! He doesn't stop looking until he finds it. Does such diligence comfort your heart when you think of this in terms of a lost loved one?

- - - - - HE MAY FIND, BUT THEY MAY NOT FOLLOW - - - -

Who does he call in to help celebrate the momentous occasion of a found sheep?

Friends *and* neighbors! This is no quiet celebration—this is a full-blown party! And the shepherd is shouting, *"Rejoice with me because I have found my lost sheep."*

Then God gives us that precious glimpse into heaven of the huge celebration that takes place every time someone repents. Don't you love imagining that celebration? What do you think the celebratory music sounds like? Think of the best celebration you've ever been a part of, and then multiply it. You still won't even come close to describing this heavenly celebration!

The next story Jesus tells is about a lost coin—and it's a particular favorite of mine. Read Luke 15:8-10 (page 798).

I can relate to coins much more easily than to sheep. Sheep are not in my frame of reference, so I have to imagine that parable. But coins? I get this picture! There have been many times when I've resorted to turning over couch cushions looking for enough money for something. I don't think I've ever called in my neighbors to celebrate with me, but I'll keep that in mind for the next time around. If you noticed, the parable is almost identical to the first one, ending with the same jubilant celebration in heaven.

What do you think Jesus is trying to get across with these two illustrations?

> LOST SINNERS ARE OF HIGH VALUE TO GOD & TO THE HEAVENLY KINGDOM

Each parable presents God as seeking the lost, and each presents the peril of being lost. Most of all, these parables illustrate the hallmark of Luke's Gospel, *"The Son of Man came to seek and save those who are lost"* (Luke 19:10, page 801).

The Lost Son

And now we come to the last parable of the three—the Parable of the Lost Son. Read Luke 15:11-32 (page 798).

Who do you believe the following characters represent?

the younger son

WORLDLY, SELF-CENTERED, BUT CAME TO HIS SENSES & GOT RIGHT WITH THE FATHER

the father

FATHER-GOD, EXPRESSING HIS PERFECT, UNCONDITIONAL LOVE

the older son *SELF-CENTERED,*

ONE WHO WAS RELYING ON HIS GOOD WORKS TO "EARN" HIS REWARD

Why did the younger son want to leave home?

HE HADN'T EXPERIENCED THE HARDSHIPS / TRIALS THAT WOULD MAKE HIM RECOGNIZE & APPRECIATE HIS NEED

Do you ever struggle with discontentment, longing to experience new things or something different?

What are some ways you can address these feelings without causing damage to yourself or your family?

REMAIN FOCUSED ON GOD'S WORD & WAYS & SO NOT TO STRAY INTO WRONG-DOING.

When the young man finally comes to his miserable senses, he makes a momentous decision. In verses 18-19, what did he do?

HE REPENTED & RETURNED HOME

The most amazing part of this story is the joy of the father when his son returned. In all the time his son was gone, the father had never ceased longing for his return. He'd been watching the road. Just imagine the joy that must have surged through the father's heart when he recognized the man walking up the pathway was his son. *"While he was still a long way off,"* it says.

What did the father do?

HE RAN TO HIS SON & EMBRACED HIM

The father was filled with love and compassion. Not a hint of "I told you so," no "looks like you got what was coming to you"— just pure forgiving, healing, joyous love. But more than forgiveness takes place here. The father even goes beyond that. What does he tell the servants to do in verses 22-23?

CLOTHE HIM & FEED HIM WITH THE BEST

Reconciliation is happening. He's giving him the best robe in the house, putting a ring on his finger and sandals on his feet. He's dressing him as he would dress a beloved son—*because he is*!

And just like in the parable, God never throws our failures in our face—He pronounces us joint-heirs with Jesus and calls for a heavenly celebration, which is what the father did. He calls the servants. "Come, come!" you can almost hear him saying. "There's a celebration to prepare. My son has come home."

And then some drama enters the picture in the form of sibling rivalry. It was probably there all along, but the circumstance brings it to a head. Put yourself in the older brother's place. How would you feel if you'd always been the good and dutiful son, working hard, picking up your brother's slack, and respecting your father's hard-earned money? Imagine coming home after a long day's work and hearing the sounds of music and celebration coming from inside the house. You see a servant hurrying by carrying a tray piled high with expensive delicacies. "What's the occasion?" you ask him. "Your brother's home!" the servant shouts over the music. "Your dad's throwing him a party!"

The older son's anger is understandable given where his focus is. It's not on his father's joy or his brother's safety. It's on himself, and as we've already seen, a self-focus only causes harm.

There are so many lessons to be gleaned from this story. Do you get the feeling the older brother's motives were wrong from the beginning? Do you think perhaps all his hard work was not based in his love and respect for his father but with an eye on what would eventually be his? Self is such a subtle enemy, isn't it? It sneaks up on us the minute we let our guard down.

However, just as the father was waiting for his wayward son and ran to meet him, so God is waiting and longing for us and runs to meet us the minute we turn our hearts toward home.

How We Deal with Money and Time

Wow! Those were three great parables, weren't they? There are a couple more parables in chapter 16, ones that teach about stewardship (how we take care of what has been given to us). These stories deal with how we manage the money and time that God has given us to use. The "Parable of the Shrewd Manager" is interesting because it uses a bad example to show us how to practice good stewardship.

Read Luke 16:1-13 (pages 798-799).

What lesson was Jesus teaching in this parable?
ONE CAN BE SHREWD IN THIS WORLD & GAIN (SO-CALLED) "FRIENDS" BUT HONEST & RIGHTEOUS LIVING IS WHAT COUNTS TO GOD

I like the way *The Message* paraphrases Jesus' words in the last part of this parable. Beginning with verse 8 it reads,

> *Now here's a surprise: The master praised the crooked manager! And why? Because he knew how to look after himself. Streetwise people are smarter in this regard than law-abiding citizens. They are on constant alert, looking for angles, surviving by their wits. I want you to be smart in the same way— but for what is right—using every adversity to stimulate you to creative survival, to concentrate your attention on the bare essentials, so you'll live, really live, and not complacently just get by on good behavior.*

I especially like the phrase, *"I want you to be smart in the same way—but for what is right—using every adversity to stimulate you to creative survival...so you'll live, really live..."*

This is exactly what Jesus is teaching us to do in this first parable on stewardship. Jesus was not commending the manager's dishonesty but his shrewdness. The manager used his present opportunity to prepare for the future.

The Bible has a lot to say about our money and possessions. God is aware of where we can be vulnerable. Before moving on to the next parable, let's look at some other verses on this topic. As you read them, note their main thought.

Proverbs 13:11 (page 489)

"EASY"/DISHONEST MONEY IS NOT APPRECIATED & IS EASILY SQUANDERED — HONEST GAIN IS VALUED & USED MORE WISELY.

Ecclesiastes 5:10 (page 507)

THE LOVE OR FOCUS ON WEALTH CAN NEVER BE SATISFIED (ALWAYS WANT MORE).

Mark 12:17 (page 773)

GIVE TO THE WORLD WHAT IS DUE — GIVE GOD WHAT IS HIS (HEART / SOUL / REVERENCE / OBEDIENCE ---)

1 Timothy 6:7-10 (pages 912-913)

BE CONTENT — DON'T GET TRAPPED INTO THE PURSUIT OF WEALTH & FAME; STAY FOCUSED ON GOD & HIS KINGDOM

1 Corinthians 16:1-2 (pages 880-881)

SET ASIDE MONEY (OR PROVISIONS) FOR GOD'S SERVICE FIRST, SO YOU CAN PARTICIPATE IN HELPING OTHERS BEYOND YOURSELF (BE A GOOD STEWARD OF WHAT GOD GIVES YOU!)

No one can serve two masters.
For you will hate one and love the other;
you will be devoted to one and despise the other.
You cannot serve both God and money.

Luke 16:13 (page 799)

Lazarus and the Rich Man

The next parable is found in Luke 16:19-31 (page 799).

What did the rich man want Abraham to do?

TO SEND LAZARUS TO COOL HIS TONGUE w/ WATER — AND TO SEND LAZARUS TO TESTIFY (FROM THE DEAD) to THE RULER'S BROTHERS TO

What do verses 23 and 26 together suggest? *SAVE THEM.*

HELL IS A REAL PLACE, SET ASIDE/RESERVED FOR THE UNSAVED — AND THERE IS NO ESCAPE.

Why wouldn't Abraham grant the rich man's request for Lazarus to talk to his family?

THE RULER'S BROTHERS WERE TOO HARDENED TO EVEN ACCEPT THE TRUTH FROM A "MIRACLE MESSENGER" — TRUTH COULDN'T PENETRATE THEIR HEARTS.

We should never forget that hell is as much of a reality as heaven. It was too late for any help to reach the rich man, but he asked for Lazarus to go back to warn his brothers (Luke 16:28). Sadly, that couldn't be done either. This brief time on earth is our only opportunity to invest in eternity!

> Seek the LORD while you can find him.
> Call on him now while he is near.

Isaiah 55:6 (page 560)

A side issue that this parable addresses is the seeming injustice of life in this world. Sometimes it seems like evil people are getting away with their evil deeds, living in luxury, while the righteous are poor and suffer hardships. What does verse 25 say?

THE WELL-TO-DO ALREADY RECEIVE THEIR REWARD IN THIS LIFE.

Locked into the confines of time, we sometimes forget that this time on earth is only a speck compared to all of eternity. Eternity is what we should be investing in now because it is *eternity*!

Sin, Faith, Duty, Gratitude, and the Coming Kingdom

Jesus was teaching His disciples these things while on their way to Jerusalem, where He knew He would be crucified. Chapter 17 takes up Jesus' teaching on sin, faith, duty, gratitude, and the coming of God's Kingdom.

Read Luke 17:1-4 (page 799).
What does it say all followers of Christ will face?

TEMPTATIONS TO SIN

What did Jesus say about the one who causes the temptation?

HIS GUILT IS COMPOUNDED FOR LEADING OTHERS INTO SIN — HE WOULD BE BETTER OFF DROWNED W/ A MILLSTONE AROUND HIS NECK

In verses 3-4, what does Jesus say He expects us to do when someone sins against us?

FORGIVE THEM

Does that last sentence stun you? What Jesus is saying is that we are to be *relentless* in giving forgiveness. The reason is simple—and it is for us, not the one asking forgiveness. If you are unforgiving, what kind of emotions are inside you? Joy? Peace? Hope? Not likely. It's more likely to be bitterness, hatred, anger. If these emotions are inside of you, who's being hurt by them? It's not the person who's sinned against you—it is you!

We not only need to forgive others because it is best for our own health, but we also need to forgive others so that we are being obedient to God. Note what the following verses say.

Matthew 18:21-22 (page 749)

"continually forgive"
("70 × 7")

Colossians 3:13 (page 904)

forgive as the Lord does

Ephesians 4:32 (page 897)

forgive as God (through Christ) forgives

What is the underlying reason why we need to forgive others?

it's an obedient + Godly behavior (our gratitude for God's forgiveness)

Yes, we have been forgiven! What wonderful news. We should forgive others because God, through Christ, has forgiven all of our sins. God's forgiveness of our sins serves as a model for us as we interact with those around us.

Read Luke 17:5-6 (page 799).
What did the disciples ask Jesus to do?

to increase their faith

If a small bit of faith can uproot and throw a tree, just imagine what big faith could do. Jesus wants us to know that faith knows no impossibilities. One of the best ways to increase our faith is by becoming familiar with God's Word. The more we know, the more we understand and believe that with God all things are possible (Luke 1:37, page 780). Let's look at some other faith-building verses. What is the key idea in each?

Matthew 21:18-22 (pages 751-752)

belief (trust/faith) is key to answered prayer

1 John 5:14-15 (pages 943-944)

we must pray according to God's will to receive what we ask

Ephesians 6:16 (page 898)

(the shield of) faith is our protection from Satan's assaults

Romans 4:19-21 (page 860)

(Abraham) trusted God's word over-and-above his (old-age) circumstances — UNWAIVERING FAITH IN GOD

A little further on in Luke is an interesting story about ten lepers. In that day, the word translated *leprosy* was used of various skin diseases. Some were more contagious and disfiguring than others. The separation and isolation commanded by Moses' Law, along with the contagion and disfigurement, made lepers complete outcasts. Read Luke 17:11-19 (page 799).

These ten lepers asked Jesus to have mercy on them. How did Jesus heal the leper in Luke 5:13 (page 785)?

Jesus touched him & told him to "be clean"

What method did Jesus use to heal these lepers in Luke 17:14?

He just told them to go present themselves to the priests (their diseases were cured on their way)

In Leviticus 14 (pages 89-91) we are told that the priest had to certify the healing of a leper (see also Luke 5:14, page 785). The ten men in Luke 17 showed faith as they actively walked to the priest, but when does it say they were healed? *ON THEIR WAY*

Can you even begin to imagine the incredible joy they felt when, as they walked, they began to notice their bodies were healing?

ASTONISHED JOY!

And here is the curious part of this story. All ten were healed! How many came back to thank Jesus?

ONLY THE ONE (SAMARITAN) "FOREIGNER"

How is it possible, when all ten of them were healed from an awful disease—a disease that had destroyed their life—that only one came back to thank Jesus?

Stop and think for a moment of all the blessings we take for granted every day. Take for instance, your beating heart. Have you ever thought to thank God that it beats so well? So many, many things we take for granted, and all of them are ours only by the grace of God.

> Let's stop right now and tell God, "Thank you." Take a few minutes to list some of the things you're thankful for that you've never acknowledged before.
>
> - CHILD IN LOVING FAMILY
> - PRIVELEGED LIFE CIRCUMSTANCES
> - HOLY SPIRIT'S DIRECTION, DRAWING ME TO CHRIST (TRUTH)
> - BIBLE BELIEVING FAITHFUL PASTOR/ CHURCH FAMILY

Parables About Prayer

In chapter 18 we find two interesting parables on prayer. Read Luke 18:1-8 (page 800).

> How is the judge described?
>
> DID NOT FEAR GOD OR CARE FOR PEOPLE

Not the kind of person you'd want to seek justice from, is he? Jesus always added interesting little twists to His stories. According to verse 5 what did the judge decide to do?

> SAW THAT SHE RECEIVED JUSTICE, DUE TO HER PERSISTANCE

Do you see the interesting contrast? An unjust judge giving justice. That's why we don't have to be afraid of circumstances that seem unfair. God is not limited by the facts of the situation. He can cause anyone to do anything even if, like this judge, they care nothing about Him or other people.

What will God do when we "*cry out to him day and night*"?

ANSWER OUR (RIGHTEOUS) PRAYERS

In closing, let's look at two examples of prayers. Read Luke 18:9-14. Use the following chart to compare the differences between the two men praying.

The Prayers of Two Men

Prayer of the Pharisee: Characteristics	Prayer of the Tax Collector: Characteristics
SELF - RIGHTEOUS	(HUMBLE) MEEK/ASHAMED
PROUD	HESATENT BEFORE GOD
BRAIZEN/BOLD	REPENTENT
BOASTFUL	SOUGHT GOD'S FORGIVENESS
SELF-JUSTIFIED DID NOT ASK FORGIVENESS	

What is the key difference between the Pharisee and the tax collector?

Humility is such an important aspect of our relationship with God—always being aware that all we have and are is from His merciful hand. The scales are so unbalanced (in our favor) because of His unmatchable, unfathomable love!

(UNCONDITIONAL)

——————— *Personal Reflection and Application* ———————

From this chapter,

I see…

I believe…

I will…

————————————————— ∾ —————————————————

Prayer

Father, you are my sun and my shield. You give me grace and glory. You will withhold no good thing from me when I do what is right. You bless me, Lord; you surround me with your shield of love (Psalm 84:11, page 452, and Psalm 5:12, page 416).

——————— *Thoughts, Notes, and Prayer Requests* ———————

8

The Close of Jesus'
Public Ministry

The young man had it all. In fact, his life defined success: young, wealthy, and in a position of authority, so that every door of opportunity was open to him. In spite of all he had, however, there was an undefined emptiness in his life. He couldn't put his finger on it, but it kept gnawing at him. *What was the purpose of all his hard work and ambition, if it all ended at death?* There must be more to life than just accruing more wealth, more influence—but what was it?

He'd been hearing a lot lately about a man called Jesus—about how He boldly challenged the thinking of the religious leaders. He'd heard about the lives He seemed to be changing as a result of His revolutionary teaching. He'd even heard that the man claimed to be the Son of God and promised eternal life to all who followed Him. *Eternal life?*

He needed to find this man they called Jesus and find out some more about what He was teaching. And actually, Jesus could benefit from knowing him too. He could put Him in touch with the right people and help Him expand His ministry. Who knew where this could lead?

Prayer

Father, thank you for sending your Son, Jesus, to live on this earth so that I could have understanding and know you, the true God. Thank you that I can now live in fellowship with you because I live in fellowship with your Son. You are the only true God, and you are eternal life (1 John 5:20, page 944).

The Treasure of the Heart

The actual story of the rich young man is told in three of the four Gospels, with each adding a detail or two. You might enjoy reading the other two accounts (Matthew 19:16-30, page 750; Mark 10:17-31, page 771) later, but for now we'll focus on Luke's account. When the young man asked, *"What should I do to inherit eternal life?"* Jesus had an interesting answer. Read Luke 18:18-20 (page 800).

From what well-known Old Testament text was Jesus quoting?

TEN COMMANDMENTS

Did you notice He didn't quote all of the Ten Commandments to the young man? Remember, on more than one occasion we have seen Jesus answer people according to their *thoughts*, not their words. Jesus knew exactly what was on the young man's heart—which meant He knew just how to answer him.

Keeping that in mind, compare Jesus' answer with the Ten Commandments (Exodus 20:3-17, page 59) listed below, and circle the ones Jesus did not quote to the young man:

1. *You must not have any other god but me.*

2. *You must not make for yourself an idol of any kind or an*

image of anything in the heavens or on the earth or in the sea. You must not bow down to them or worship them.

3. *You must not misuse the name of the Lord your God.*

4. *Remember to observe the Sabbath day by keeping it holy.*

5. *Honor your father and mother.*

6. *You must not murder.*

7. *You must not commit adultery.*

8. *You must not steal.*

9. *You must not testify falsely against your neighbor.*

10. *You must not covet anything or anyone that belongs to your neighbor* (paraphrase).

The rich man quickly told Jesus that he'd kept all the commandments Jesus had listed, but Jesus had one other thing to say. Read Luke 18:21-30 (pages 800-801). What did He say the rich young man still needed to give up?

SELL EVERYTHING, GIVE MONEY TO THE POOR & FOLLOW JESUS

A Christian's wealth belongs to God and is to be used as He directs. Discipleship means laying no further claims to our possessions as our own, but putting them entirely into God's hands. We are to lay aside personal excesses to provide for the needs of others.

Our material possessions—even our lack of material possessions—can cause great spiritual conflict within us. We tend to spend far more time focusing on that aspect of our lives than on God and His promise to supply everything we need (Philippians 4:19, page 901). We enjoy watching our bank account grow or despair watching it shrink. We let our assets' value determine our level of peace and contentment, rather than God.

> The rich young man was unable to comprehend embracing something (even eternal life!) to a greater degree than he did his wealth. Compare his attitude to Peter's attitude in Luke 18:28 (page 801).
>
> *WE HAVE LEFT EVERYTHING*

Our lives will be much more satisfying and fulfilling if we can learn to hold our possessions loosely. There is an eloquent passage of Scripture on this very subject. Read 1 Timothy 6:6-10 (pages 912-913).

> How does it define great wealth?
>
> *A TEMPTATION & TRAP*

> Contentment is a challenging attitude in today's culture. What is the biggest obstacle to contentment in your life?
>
> *TOO MUCH STUFF*

> What attitude shift can you cultivate to combat your discontentment in this area?
>
>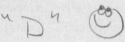

Verses 9 and 10 in 1 Timothy 6 are so blunt it's almost scary, but, again, God our Creator knows where we can be weak. What does it say about people whose focus is on "getting more"?

THEY FALL INTO TEMPTATION. & A TRAP & INTO MANY FOOLISH & HARMFUL DESIRES WHICH CAN BRING RUIN & DESTRUCTION

Do these verses speak of joy at any level? How about satisfaction or fulfillment? No. They speak of ruin, destruction, evil, and many sorrows. Why do you think the pursuit of wealth more often diminishes life rather than enhances it?

WRONG FOCUS — TOO BUSY DREAMING UP SCHEMES TO GET MORE; NOT ENOUGH TIME REALLY LIVING (TOTAL LACK OF CONTENTMENT OR SATISFACTION)

No matter what aspect of life we're talking about, it always boils down to the same question. What does your heart treasure most? The further down the list God is moved, the less satisfying your life will be.

Into the middle of all this talk about focusing on wealth, Jesus plops a fascinating statement. Read Luke 18:27.

Where in Luke did we read a similar verse?

It was when the angel appeared to Mary and told her that she, a virgin, would give birth to God's Son (Luke 1:37). Now Jesus is saying the same thing in regard to wealth and eternity. In this context, what do you think He means by that?

GOD, THRU JESUS, CAN SAVE EVEN THE WEALTHY IF THEY REPENT — GOD'S HOLY SPIRIT MAY DRAW OR GUIDE PEOPLE TO SALVATION

As strong as the allure of the world is, God is stronger. His love can draw us to Him against incredible odds! Jesus winds up His teaching on this subject with a wonderful promise. He tells them that anyone who gives up whatever comes before their love of God *"will be repaid many times over in this life, and will have eternal life in the world to come"* (Luke 18:30, page 801).

Knowing this, is there any way at all that we can lose—either in this life or in eternity—by putting God first?

NO ♡

Near the end of chapter 18 Jesus again prepares His disciples for the devastating upheaval that will soon come into their lives. Read Luke 18:31-34 (page 801).

Did you notice how detailed Jesus was about the coming events? Jesus had talked to them before about what would happen, but again the disciples could not comprehend what He told them. Why do you think they didn't understand?

THE MEANING WAS HIDDEN FROM THEM (BECAUSE THEY MIGHT HAVE TRIED TO PREVENT JESUS FROM GOING

The Encounter with Zacchaeus

The nineteenth chapter of Luke begins with a beloved Bible story that every child who's gone to Sunday school has heard and probably even sung about. It's the story of Zacchaeus, a man who had several strikes against him when we first meet him. He was a short man, so he'd probably put up with a fair amount of hurtful comments in his life.

Our stature is something we have no control over, but Zacchaeus added to his trouble by becoming a tax collector, something he did have control over. That choice led him to be a social outcast. People hated tax collectors because they considered them traitors who worked for the Romans, the hated occupiers of Israel. And they were notoriously dishonest, overcharging on the taxes they collected for the Roman government. Zacchaeus was no exception, and he'd become very wealthy as a result. Remember our earlier example of how wealth does not equal joy? Zacchaeus is a prime example.

Read Luke 19:1-7 (page 801). What caught your interest in this passage?

ZACCHAEUS RECOGNIZED HIS SINFULNESS & IMMEDIATELY OFFERED REPENTENCE & "REPAYMENT" TO THOSE HE HAD WRONGED. HE DEMONSTRATED A HEART FOR _____

Can you imagine Zacchaeus' shock to have Jesus call him by name? He not only called him by name but He invited Himself over. Actually, Jesus didn't just invite Himself—He said He *"must"* be a guest in his home. This is surprising on so many levels—not the least of which is the fact that Zacchaeus was despised by Jericho society. His house was the last place people expected Jesus to go.

According to verse 6, what was Zacchaeus' reaction?

IMMEDIATE INVITATION TO JESUS

According to verse 7, what was everyone else's reaction?

MURMERING DISPLEASURE AT JESUS' CHOICE OF COMPANION

Oh, my! People are always quick to grumble, aren't they? And they were probably envious as well. Jesus, after all, was a famous person around those parts! But Jesus wasn't there for fame. He was there because He knew Zacchaeus had a date with destiny. We are not made privy to the conversation that took place between the two. We only know Zacchaeus was forever changed.

Read verses 8-10.

What evidence do we have for his change of heart?

HE IMMEDIATELY REPENTED & OFFERED RESTITUTION TO THOSE HE HAD WRONGED — JESUS REPLIED "SALVATION HAD COME".

Suddenly, as a result of his encounter with Jesus, Zacchaeus' wealth lost its hold on him. (Remember? With God, all things are possible!) All he wanted now was to walk in God's favor. Zacchaeus' true repentance from his former way of life is also seen in his desire to make restitution to all whom he'd cheated—four times over, no less! This was a changed man. That's what true salvation does—it changes us, it opens up our hearts and our hands, and it turns our focus to God first, above all else.

What I like most about Zacchaeus is his enthusiasm. He enthusiastically found a way to see Jesus. Didn't you sense his excitement as he ran ahead of the crowd in order to find a tree to climb so he'd have a better vantage point? When Jesus looked up and, in essence, said, "Ready or not, here I come!" Zacchaeus enthusiastically welcomed Him. Finally, when Jesus showed him a better way of life, Zacchaeus enthusiastically turned from his old ways and embraced Jesus. That's the kind of enthusiasm I want to have when it comes to my relationship with Jesus!

According to Luke 19:10 (page 801), what did Jesus come to do?

seek & save the lost

Jesus' Entry into Jerusalem

As Jesus and His disciples got closer to Jerusalem, excitement was building. Read Luke 19:28-34 (page 802).

So many questions come to mind in this short passage. What questions did it raise for you? *WHY DID JESUS NEED THE COLT*
- *DID THE 2 DISCIPLES QUESTION WHETHER THINGS WOULD BE AS JESUS SAID (AND, YET, THEY WENT!).*
- *WEREN'T THEY CONCERNED THEY MIGHT BE ACCUSED OF "STEALING" THE COLT?*
- *WHEN THINGS TURNED OUT AS JESUS HAD PREDICTED, DID THEY MARVEL AT IT?*

AND WHY AN UNRIDDEN ONE?

It's interesting that the owner of the donkey didn't question the disciples once they told him, *"The Lord needs it."*

And now the terrible drama begins in earnest. Read Luke 19:35-38 (page 802). What do you notice taking place?
- *THRONGS OF PEOPLE EAGERLY AWAITING HIM*
- *THEY PRAISED GOD FOR HIM (CROWD OF DISCIPLES)*

These verses recount a very significant event as Jesus approaches Jerusalem on the back of a donkey. In biblical times, when a king visited a place for peaceful purposes, he rode a donkey. If he came to make war, he rode a horse. Jesus was coming as the Prince of Peace, so he rode an animal that symbolized peace. He presented Himself as the Messiah so that people could make their choice to accept or reject Him. This very event was prophesied in Zechariah 9:9 (page 724).

Jesus had entered Jerusalem many times before without public notice. Now, though, He allowed the acclaim of the crowds because He knew this would start the sequence of events that would take Him to the cross. The crowds following Jesus recognized Him as the Messiah. They spread their garments on His path as they would do for a king. They also sang a part of Psalm 118 (pages 467-468), which speaks of the deliverance God was sending.

Try to imagine what Jesus' thoughts must have been as He rode into the city with people laying their garments on the ground in front of Him, praising Him as their King. He knew this response would be short-lived. Very soon it would be replaced with hatred and rejection. Very soon He would face the purpose for which He had come to earth—His innocent death for our guilty lives.

The next two verses are fascinating. Read Luke 19:39-40 (page 802).

What did Jesus say would happen if He stopped the people from praising Him?

THE STONES (NATURE) WOULD CRY OUT.

Think of it! "*The stones along the road would burst into cheers!*" The crowds continued cheering, but Jesus' heartache and dread were growing within Him—not just because of what He knows He is facing. His dread is for the future of His beloved Jerusalem and the Jewish people, because they refused to recognize Him as their Messiah. Read Luke 19:41-44. What breaks Jesus' heart?

JERUSALEM (ISRAEL) ACKNOWLEDGED JESUS AS "KING," BUT NOT AS THEIR PROMISED MESSIAH — THEIR APOSTACY WOULD BRING THEIR RUIN & DOWNFALL.

Sorrow and Anger

Verse 42 is especially heart-wrenching. Are there any more devastating words than "*But now it is too late*"? They had lost their opportunity to welcome Him as Messiah. No wonder Jesus wept. Such a terrible price He was paying, only to be rejected.

Once inside the city, Jesus went to the Temple. Read Luke 19:45-48 (page 802). What did Jesus do?

JESUS DROVE OUT THE MONEY-
CHANGERS & SELLERS OF SACRIFICIAL
ANIMALS

One other time, a similar incident occurred. Read John 2:13-17 (page 810).

Both incidents occurred during the Passover season, when people came to the Temple from near and far to pay their Temple tax and to offer their sacrifices. Since the people came from different countries, their currencies had to be changed to the Hebrew coin. Money changers took advantage of the situation to make excessive profits. The merchants also made a good profit on the doves, cattle, and sheep they sold for sacrificial purposes. Once again, their focus was skewed and it distracted the people from God and made the Temple like any stall in the marketplace.

Interestingly, the first incident took place at the beginning of Jesus' ministry and the last one took place at the end of His ministry. In fact, the final incident was Jesus' last public act in front of the nation of Israel prior to the cross.

Jesus is now facing His final days on earth. Soon He will be free of the limitations of His earthly body and raised in a glorified body. Soon He will have defied death in a spectacular display of unparalleled power, but first He had to endure Calvary.

One Last Parable

Jesus had one last parable to tell—one the religious leaders clearly understood. He told it to them after a group of leading priests, teachers of religious law, and elders came to Him with a question. *"They demanded, 'By what authority are you doing all these things? Who gave you the right?'"* (Luke 20:2, page 802).

Once again, Jesus did not argue with them. He knew their motives. Instead He told them a parable. Read Luke 20:9-18 (pages 802-803).

This parable is actually an allegory that these leaders understood. They knew the vineyard represented Israel.

Who did the owner of the vineyard represent?

FATHER GOD

Who were the tenant farmers?

TEACHERS OF THE LAW, CHIEF PRIESTS & ISRAEL, WHO WOULD SOON REJECT JESUS' POSITION AS MESSIAH (THEY ALREADY DID, TAKING JESUS AS "KING" INSTEAD)

Who were the servants the owner sent?

THE PROPHETS

Who was the owner's son?

JESUS

What did the tenant farmers do with the son?

THEY KILLED HIM

Jesus was telling the religious leaders exactly what was on their minds. He was telling them He knew they were going to kill Him and that God was going to permit it. He was also letting them know this would not destroy God's plan. Instead, it would cause His purpose to be carried out because, by allowing them to kill Jesus, it would make salvation possible for all people.

The stone the religious leaders rejected as worthless turned out to be the most important of all. Jesus Christ is that cornerstone. He is the foundation stone that everything is built on in our lives (1 Corinthians 3:11, page 871).

Personal Reflection and Application

From this chapter,

I see…

I believe…

I will…

✁

Prayer

Father, I am so grateful that you are not slow in keeping your promise, as some understand slowness. Instead you are patient with everyone, not wanting anyone to be destroyed, but for everyone to repent (2 Peter 3:9, page 939).

Thoughts, Notes, and Prayer Requests

9

Jesus' Death and Resurrection

I almost missed the sign on the crowded street. It was quite small and was placed high on the stone wall above my head: *Via Dolorosa*. In spite of the heat radiating off the stones, I shivered looking up at it. *This was it.* This narrow, twisting, cobbled street was the one Jesus stumbled down on the last agonizing day of His life as the price of my redemption was being hammered out.

The loud shouts of street vendors selling their wares, the raised voices of a dozen different tour guides vying for their group's attention, the swirling conversations of tourists pushing against me faded away as I stopped dead in my tracks and let myself be absorbed by the remnants of a palpable horror still present even in the cacophony of this modern world.

I'd expected more—a grand avenue perhaps, a broad vista—but the Via Dolorosa was far from either. It was crushingly narrow—so narrow I couldn't imagine how my Savior pushed His way through the pressing crowds with the rough-hewn cross jarring against His torn flesh. I stood rooted in place, paralyzed by my part in what had taken place here.

Narrow is the way that leads to life. The thought came as a whisper, a gentle nudge to keep moving. I shook off the darkness and took a step forward, and another, quickly, eagerly rejoining the pace of the crowd around me. I had a destination to reach—the empty tomb—and this narrow street would take me there. The Via Dolorosa led Jesus to His death more than 2000 years ago, yet because of His death, today we are able to have eternal life through Him. Praise God!

Prayer

Jesus, I do not know how to adequately acknowledge my gratitude for your willingness to be pierced for my rebellion, crushed for my sins. Jesus, you were beaten so I could be whole and whipped so I could be healed. So today I confess with my mouth that you are Lord. I believe in my heart that you were raised from the dead, so that I can be saved (Isaiah 53:5, page 559, and Romans 10:9, page 864).

The religious leaders were relentless in their attempts to trick Jesus into answering their questions in such a way that they could accuse Him of blasphemy. They were determined to kill Him, but thought they would have to wait until after the Passover feast because of His popularity. However, opportunity came from an unexpected source. Read Luke 22:1-6 (page 804).

Who does verse 3 say entered Judas Iscariot?

IT ~~DOESN'T~~ SAY   SATAN

What did the leading priests and the captains of the Temple guard promise to give Judas in return?

MONEY

Why wouldn't they arrest Jesus in front of the crowds? What is the significance of this?

THEY FEARED AN UPRISING — JESUS WAS (AT THAT TIME) POPULAR AMONG THE PEOPLE (AS THEIR KING) ⟨RULERS DO NOT ALWAYS DO WHAT THE PEOPLE WANT — OR WHAT'S BEST FOR THE PEOPLE⟩

Why should we *not* fear people?

WE SHOULD KEEP OUR FOCUS ON GOD AND HIS TRUTH (RIGHT IS RIGHT, REGARDLESS OF WHETHER "RIGHT" IS OR IS NOT POPULAR)

Judas had the opportunity to know Jesus as only a few men did, but something kept him from fully committing his life to Him. It is not enough simply to know about Jesus. It's not enough to hang out with other believers or even to pray or read our Bibles. Salvation comes only when we decide to exchange our way of life for Jesus' way of life. We accept what Christ did as the entire work needed to satisfy the wrath of God and pay the penalty for our sins.

The Final Passover Celebration

The Passover celebration commemorates when God led the Israelites out of Egypt under the leadership of Moses. It is a significant holiday for the Jews, and Jesus looked forward to celebrating it with His disciples. He sent Peter and John ahead to prepare the meal. His instructions to them are reminiscent of when He sent some disciples ahead to find Him a donkey. Read Luke 22:7-13 (page 804).

What city were Peter and John supposed to travel to?

JERUSALEM (IMPLIED)

Who was supposed to meet them?

A MAN CARRYING A JAR OF WATER

What does Jesus refer to Himself as in verse 11?

"THE TEACHER"

Isn't it interesting that the room was already set up? And just like the owner of the donkey, this man seemed neither surprised nor put off by the request.

Each Passover meal had a specific itinerary for the evening:

- opening prayer for blessing

- recitation of the story of the Passover from Exodus 12 (pages 52-53)

- singing of Psalms 113 and 114 (page 466)

- eating the sacrificed lamb, bitter herbs, unleavened bread, and wine—all of which represented various aspects of Israel's journey out of Egypt

- concluding prayer

- chanting of Psalms 115–118 (pages 467-468)

At this Passover meal with His disciples, however, Jesus gave new meaning to the bread and wine. Read Luke 22:14-30 (pages 804-805).

What did Jesus say the bread represented?

HIS BODY, GIVEN FOR US

What did the wine represent?

THE NEW COVENANT IN HIS BLOOD

According to verse 19, why are we supposed to eat the bread and drink the wine?

IN REMEMBRANCE OF JESUS' SACRIFICE FOR US

As on other occasions, when Jesus spoke of His coming death, the disciples didn't comment. The conversation that took place around the table that night is intriguing. Jesus is talking to them about His coming suffering, but they don't pick up on anything until He mentions that one of them is going to betray Him. They start asking each other who it could possibly be. Then suddenly they move on to an entirely different subject.

According to verse 24, what do they discuss next?

THEIR INDIVIDUAL "IMPORTANCE" TO THE MINISTRY

Read Luke 22:31-34. Finally, Jesus' words begin to sink in, and Peter assures Jesus that he is willing to following Him to the death. However, Jesus knows Peter better than Peter knows himself.

What does Jesus tell him in verse 34?

PETER WILL DENY KNOWING JESUS THREE TIMES BEFORE THE ROOSTER CROWS

Jesus' Prayer and His Arrest

After the meal was finished, the group walked to the Mount of Olives. What did Jesus tell them to do in verse 40?

PRAY YOU WON'T GO INTO TEMPTATION

Twice that night Jesus told them to pray so they wouldn't be overcome with temptation. Telling God what we need is always important, but when facing a severe trial, it is essential. Jesus knew exactly what His beloved disciples would be facing in the next hours. He knew that there would be great temptation to take the easy way out, to run away and hide. He wanted to infuse them with strength and courage, and He knew that prayer would put them into contact with the God of all power.

Can you think of a time when praying to God gave you great strength or courage to face something?

AN ANGEL FROM HEAVEN

It is exactly what Jesus did to strengthen Himself for what lay ahead. His prayer is an agonizing mix of dread and willingness as He pleaded for a way out, even as He yielded Himself to the Father's higher purpose. Read verses 41-46.

What strengthened Jesus in verse 43?

AN ANGEL FROM HEAVEN

What was the result of Jesus being strengthened? How can this truth impact our prayer lives?

What do you think Jesus meant when He told them to get up and pray so that they would not give in to temptation?

PRAY THEY WON'T FALL INTO
TEMPTATION TO DENY JESUS

Think of the terrible emotional agony passing between heaven and earth at this point—even before the physical agony has begun. Think of the effect Jesus' prayer had on His Father. This had been the plan from the beginning of time—but oh, what a chasm there can be between plan and reality! It overwhelms me to think that no Person of the Trinity wavered in His love for humanity—even knowing how many people would ultimately reject their unfathomable love.

Read Luke 22:47-51. Suddenly, Jesus and His followers were aware of an approaching crowd of people. Let's step into this terrible picture for a moment to grasp it more fully. It takes the disciples a moment to realize it is Judas who is leading the crowd. Imagine as they stand there and watch him walk up to Jesus and kiss His cheek. How long did it take for all the pieces to fall into place, for them to realize their brother—with whom they'd shared this incredible three-year journey—had turned traitor? All the things Jesus had been telling them, that they'd tried to avoid thinking about, suddenly became crystal clear. Their beloved Lord was in danger.

Without warning, one of the disciples drew his sword and lashed out at the nearest man, slicing off his ear. Jesus quickly intervened. *"No more of this,"* He said. He touched the man's ear and healed him.

Now stop right here for a moment. A miracle had just occurred! And yet it appears to go by unnoticed.

Do you think it actually did? Did it give even one of the men in the mob pause? Surely it had to have caught someone's attention, or were they too riled up to even notice?

Read verses 52-53 (page 805). How did Jesus respond to the leaders of the crowd?

HE POINTED OUT THEIR DECEIT IN TAKING HIM SECRETLY, WHEN HE WAS ALWAYS AVAILABLE PUBLICLY IN THE TEMPLE COURTS. (AND HE GAVE UP PEACEFULLY, WITH NO NEED OF THEIR SWORDS & CLUBS)

The Unjust Trial

Read verses 54-62 (pages 805-806). They arrested Jesus and took Him to the home of the high priest. Some of the guards lit a fire in the courtyard. They gathered around for warmth, as they waited to see what would happen next. Peter joined them at the fire and a servant girl suddenly pointed to him.

Oh, does your heart break for Peter, who just hours before had made his rash promise to follow Jesus to the death? Imagine how his heart was pierced when his eyes met Jesus' eyes. And what makes it even worse is the thought that I would likely have responded exactly as Peter did. How do you think you would have responded on a night so fraught with fear and betrayal and uncertainty? Put yourself around the fire pit, listening to the conversation.

Would you have defended Jesus or remained silent?

IF I SPOKE UP IT WOULD PROBABLY HAVE BEEN SOMETHING "WISHY-WASHY" LIKE, "IS HE REALLY SO BAD ---?"

Read Luke 22:63-71 (page 806).

The religious leaders who had Jesus arrested held a meeting of some of the Jewish religious Council, which was called the Sanhedrin. This Council had 71 members, but it took only 23 members to constitute a quorum.[1]

They followed some of their laws and rules—however, the laws and rules that went against their purpose they broke. It is so easy to manipulate our definition of right and wrong when there is something we are determined to have or do.

These men went to outrageous lengths in order to find Jesus guilty. Early on they quit seeking justice because they wanted Him dead, no matter what laws they had to break to make it happen.

The entire proceedings were unlawful. Some illegalities committed by the enemies of Jesus include:

- The arrest was without authority of law, and therefore illegal.

- Annas, before whom Jesus was first taken for examination, was a mere politician without jurisdiction whatsoever.

- The Sanhedrin was unlawfully assembled for these reasons: The Hebrew laws prohibited such a meeting in the nighttime, or on a Friday, or during the great Feast of the Passover.

- Jesus was first accused of blasphemy, but when before Pilate, the charge was changed to sedition, without notice to the prisoner, or anyone.

- Jesus was denied an opportunity to obtain His witnesses who would have testified in His behalf.

- No person could be found guilty upon his own confession of guilt, alone.

- There had to be at least two witnesses to testify in support of the charge against the accused; and their testimony must agree as to all the material facts involved.

- The trial could not lawfully have been concluded in a single day.

- The Roman conquerors had long before taken from the Sanhedrin its authority to sentence anyone to suffer the death penalty.

- A unanimous verdict of guilty rendered by the Jewish court had the effect of an acquittal.

- The members of the Sanhedrin were definitely disqualified to try Jesus because of enmity toward the accused.

- The merits of Jesus' defense were completely ignored by the Sanhedrin.

- Pilate, as the Roman governor, having stated four times that Jesus was not guilty of any wrong, should have released Him, instead of delivering Him over to the mob for crucifixion.

- The condemnation of the Christ, resulting in His death on the cross, was permitted to be done without a lawful judgment of conviction.

- The members of the Great Sanhedrin, though learned in the law, deliberately and spitefully ignored every existing Hebrew law that had been enacted for the protection of the innocent.

Jesus Is Sentenced to Death

Because the Jewish council, the Sanhedrin, could not publicly carry out the death sentence they had pronounced, they had to go to

[handwritten margin note: SIGNS OF CURRENT TIMES — UNLAWFUL "LEADERSHIP" CATERING TO "POLITICAL CORRECTNESS" RATHER THAN LAW AND TRUTH]

a civil court. They took Jesus to Pilate in spite of having no civil charge against Him. Read Luke 23:1-25 (page 806).

Why did Herod want to see Jesus?

TO SEE JESUS PERFORM A MIRACLE

What did Herod and his soldiers do to Jesus before they sent Him back to Pilate?

RIDICULED & MOCKED JESUS & PUT ON AN "ELEGANT" ROBE AS A SHOW OF "ROYALTY"

Why do you think Pilate and Herod suddenly became friends?

BY BEING AGREEABLE/FRIENDLY WITH ONE ANOTHER, THEY (JOINTLY) WERE ABLE TO GET OUT OF THE RESPONSIBILITY OF THE SITUATION

What do you infer from Pilate choosing to flog Jesus even *(POLITICALLY CORRECT BY PERVERSE AGREEMENT)* though he found Him innocent?

HE HOPED TO PLACATE THE CROWD WITHOUT CONDEMNING JESUS TO DEATH

Did anyone ever find a legitimate reason to kill Jesus?

NO

Jesus suffered so much injustice. If you think there is no one who can understand the injustice you've endured, think again. He knows exactly what it feels like! He understands when no one else does!

The physical abuse and punishment Jesus suffered as He was passed back and forth between the rulers was staggering. A prophecy of His torment, written hundreds of years prior to the actual event, paints a horrifying but accurate picture. Read Isaiah 52:14 (page 559).

People who reject Jesus today are as guilty as those who insisted on His death then. The truth is, every human being shares in the guilt. But thanks to the incredible love and mercy of Jesus, our Messiah and Savior, we do not have to answer for our guilt. If we have trusted in Him, He has proclaimed us innocent!

Judgment was passed on Jesus in spite of His innocence, and a death sentence was pronounced: death by crucifixion—the cruelest form of death used by the Romans. The condemned were normally required to carry their own crosses. However, the severe abuse and beating had left Jesus' back so raw and His body so weak that He collapsed under the weight of the cross. A bystander who had just arrived in the city was forced to carry Jesus' cross for Him. Read Luke 23:26-27 (page 806).

While the Bible does not say for certain, we can imagine what this might have been like for Simon from Cyrene. You are coming into town on that day, planning only to take care of business and head back home. You have no idea of what is taking place. You see the crowds, hear their intense mixture of hatred and grief, and wonder what's going on. The thought of a crucifixion crosses your mind, for the Romans are notorious for such things. You consider turning back, saving your errands for another day. You are trying to move away from the crowd when suddenly a Roman official pulls you aside and orders you to carry the cross for the criminal being crucified.

Simon would not have known what was happening if he had just come into town on that day. Do you think his life was changed from that point on? Did he tell his story every chance he got of how he carried the cross for the man who claimed to be God? Or did he keep the news to himself, overwhelmed by the part he played in that terrible day? As he struggled beneath the weight of the cross, knowing what lay ahead for the man beside him, did he recognize Jesus to be his Savior?

The Crucifixion

When the procession reached the place reserved for public execution outside the city walls, Jesus was nailed to the cross. Read *LUKE 23:* verses 32-34 (pages 806-807). How did Jesus respond to the crucifixion?

HE ASKED GOD'S FORGIVENESS ON HIS PERSECUTERS

Even in the midst of terrible suffering, Jesus' first thought was for the people carrying out the deed.

Read verses 35-38. How did the crowd react?

SNEERED, MOCKED & RIDICULED HIM

It is hard to fathom such barbarism in our "cleaned-up" culture today. But the reality is, we are just as guilty and barbaric. Jesus' name is still mocked in casual, angry, and emotional conversations. The fact that many consider Him to be nothing more than a historical figure is the worst of mockery. What about the religious belief that claims He is one of many ways to God?

The awful truth is—nothing has changed! We have dressed up our barbaric ways to make them more palatable. God, however, sees through it all—right straight into our hearts. He knows where we stand in the crowd.

Two other men were crucified with Jesus that day—both criminals, deserving of death. But each reacted to Jesus' crucifixion differently from the other. Read verses 39-43.

What were the two reactions of the men?

- *ONE ACKNOWLEDGED HIS SIN & ASKED JESUS FOR HIS MERCY*
- *THE OTHER SPOKE INSULTS AT JESUS & CHALLENGED HIM TO (MIRACULOUSLY) SAVE HIMSELF AND THEM*

How did Jesus respond to the criminal who said he had done nothing wrong?

DID NOT RESPOND

Jesus' mercy is unbelievable. Even at the point of death Jesus welcomes the believing criminal into the Kingdom of God and blesses him with eternal life. That same mercy is available to every single one of us. If you have not yet made the choice to follow Jesus, now is the time. With the picture of the price He paid for you fresh in your mind, exchange your old way of life for the new life He procured for you on the cross. (You may want to read the section "Know God" near the end of this study—pages 185-187). All of heaven is waiting in anticipation of celebrating your choice.

Jesus on the Cross

According to Mark 15:25 (page 777), what time of day was Jesus nailed to the cross?

"THIRD HOUR" (THEIR DAYS BEGAN AT 6:AM, SO IT WAS AT 9:AM)

Now read Luke 23:44-45 (page 807). What happened at noon?

DARKNESS CAME OVER THE WHOLE LAND (@ "6TH HOUR" = NOON).

How long did the darkness last?

UNTIL THE 9th HOUR — IT LASTED 3 HOURS (TO 3:PM)

Darkness in the middle of the day! How frightening do you think it must have been as the sky grew darker and darker? How do you think today's media would have explained such a phenomenon to the public?

A MYSTERIOUS FLUKE OF NATURE

From this timeline, we know that Jesus remained on the cross for six hours or more. While He hung on that cross, bearing our sins, something wonderful happened. In Christ, God reconciled us to Himself. The cross made salvation available to everyone!

During those six hours, Jesus made seven different statements. Read the following verses and note what He said:

Luke 23:34 (page 807)

"FATHER FORGIVE THEM — — —

Luke 23:43 (page 807) *(TO THE REPENTANT THIEF)*

"— TODAY YOU WILL BE WITH ME IN PARADISE."

John 19:26-27 (page 827)

TO MOTHER MARY (RE: DISCIPLE JOHN): "— HERE IS YOUR SON."
(TO JOHN RE: MARY) "— HERE IS YOUR MOTHER."

Matthew 27:46 (page 760)

MY GOD, MY GOD, WHY HAVE YOU FORSAKEN ME?"

John 19:28 (page 827)

"I AM THIRSTY."

John 19:30 (page 827)

"IT IS FINISHED."

Luke 23:46 (page 807)

"FATHER, INTO YOUR HANDS I COMMIT MY SPIRIT."

Jesus did not die as a victim; He died as a victor. He is the very Source of Life. People did not take His life from Him—He gave His life freely. He had power over life and death, and He died willingly. He died voluntarily—for you and for me.

Read John 10:18 (page 819).

Jesus died because He loved us. He took our punishment because of His great love. We cannot understand love like that, but it should inspire our wholehearted love and devotion for Him.

Jesus died around three o'clock in the afternoon. Read Luke 23:47-49. How did the crowd react to His death?

they beat their breasts (in fear + anguish) and went away

Can you imagine the horrible, sickening feeling that must have been in the pit of the officer's stomach when he realized the truth? What about the inconsolable grief of the people who now fully realized what they'd just witnessed?

According to Jewish law, Jesus' followers had until only six o'clock to bury the body before the official Passover Feast Day began.

Read Luke 23:50-56 (page 807).

Who was Joseph from Arimathea? *LUKE 22:66*

a member of the Council of the elders of the people

What did the women from Galilee do?

they followed Joseph to the tomb so they knew where Jesus body was laid — then went home + prepared burial spices

The Resurrection

Jesus had told His disciples several times that He would rise from the dead (Luke 9:22, page 790, and Luke 18:33, page 801), but this was understandably beyond their comprehension. After He died, they were devastated. The man they'd followed for three years, who had irrevocably changed their lives forever, was gone.

Meanwhile, the enemies of Jesus remembered Jesus talking about His resurrection, and they didn't want to take any chances. Read Matthew 27:62-66 (page 760).

WHAT ABOUT LAZARUS, etc.?

What precautions did they take?

put a seal over the stone entrance door and posted a guard

Isn't it ironic that the disbelievers put round-the-clock guards at the tomb, but the believers never considered waiting around—just to see? They'd both heard the same things and took very different actions.

And now, at last—the dark hopelessness of death is about to be defied! Read Luke 24:1-11 (page 807), and Matthew 28:1-6 (page 760).

What did the women come to the tomb to do?

to prepare Jesus' "dead" body with the spices they brought

What happened to the guards?

From fear of the angels they fainted as-if dead

What did the women do once they remembered what Jesus had said?

they ran to tell the news to the disciples + others who were with them

There are at least four witnesses to the empty tomb. Read the following verses. Who are the witnesses?

Matthew 28:11-13 (page 760)

• the guards of the tomb

LUKE 24:10 { *• MARY MAGDALENE, JOANNA, MARY (MOTHER OF JAMES) & OTHERS*

Luke 24:1-3 (page 807)

THE WOMEN WHO ACCOMPANIED JESUS FROM GALILEE

Luke 24:12 (page 807)

PETER

John 20:3-10 (page 828)

(PETER) & JOHN

What does the last passage say about the linen wrappings?

they were in strips

Go back to John 20:9 (page 828). What does it say?

the disciples still did not understand Jesus had to rise from the dead

Look at Matthew 28:11-13 (page 760) again.

There is strong historical evidence that springs from the Roman and Jewish officials admitting that the tomb was empty and bribing the guards to lie. They were admitting a fact that was not in their favor, proving the fact was genuine. Historians call this "positive evidence from a hostile source." It's interesting to note that no early source, friendly or hostile, ever claimed that the tomb was not empty. For at least the first four centuries after Jesus' resurrection, even hostile sources agreed that the tomb was empty.[2]

Meeting the Risen Jesus

Read Luke 24:13-24 (pages 807-808).

Can't you just picture this scene? Can't you feel the emotion of those two people, their surprise at meeting someone who hadn't heard all that had happened?

Read Luke 24:25-34 (page 808).

According to verse 27, what did Jesus do after the two said that the tomb was empty?

He explained it all from scripture (prophecies)

At what moment did they recognize Jesus?

as He began to serve the "communion" / breaking of the bread

What did they say to each other when Jesus disappeared from their sight?

Weren't our hearts burning within us as He spoke and revealed scripture to us (excited by the hope!)

How much time had passed before the two started back to Jerusalem to tell the disciples and others about their experience?

they left at once

Don't you love it? "*Within the hour*" they turned around. They hardly took time to catch their breath!

Read Luke 24:35-43 (page 808).

What happened while they were telling everyone about seeing Jesus?

Jesus came & stood among them — revealed Himself in physical form — He ate fish with them

How did Jesus prove to them that He was not a ghost?

(all the foregoing — He allowed them to touch Him)

Can you feel the electricity in the air? Extreme shock and disbelief. Breathtaking joy. Their Savior, friend, and Messiah was alive! Death did not win. Everything He promised came to pass—just as He had said.

According to Acts 1:3 (page 830) Jesus continued appearing to the disciples and His followers for 40 days before ascending into heaven. This time when Jesus left them, the disciples had a very different reaction. Read Luke 24:50-53 (page 808). What did they do?

they worshiped Jesus & returned to the Temple & stayed there, praising God

The Bible records 15 appearances of Jesus after His resurrection. Luke records three of the main ones. When all of these reports are put together, we have a more complete picture of Jesus' appearances after His resurrection. Below are 11 more instances we haven't yet read about. Who did He appear to in each account?

John 20:11-18 (page 828)

Mary of Magdala

John 20:24-29 (page 828)

the disciples and Thomas

John 21:1-14 (page 829) *disciples:*
Simon Peter, Thomas (Didymus), Nathanael (2) sons of Zebedee and (2) others

Matthew 28:16-20 (page 760)

The 11 disciples

1 Corinthians 15:5 (page 879)

to Peter, then to the 12 apostles

1 Corinthians 15:6 (page 879)

over 500 "brothers" (believers) at one time

1 Corinthians 15:7 (page 879)

to James, then all the apostles

Acts 1:3-5 (page 830)

to His chosen apostles

Acts 7:55-56 (page 836)

Stephen (at His stoning) saw Jesus in Heaven

Acts 9:1-9 (pages 837-838)

Saul – on road to Damascus (bright/blinding light – and voice)

Revelation 1:1,13-18 (page 949), and Revelation 19:11-16 (page 960) *Apostle John (through vision of angel)*

Jesus' Final Message on Earth

Before His ascension, Jesus commissioned His disciples to continue the work He'd begun with them. The Great Commission, as it is referred to, is recorded in three of the Gospels. Read each passage and sum up the emphasis of the three.

Matthew 28:19-20 (page 760)

go make disciples of all nations, baptize in name of FATHER, SON & HOLY SPIRIT, teach obedience to law/commands He gave

Mark 16:15 (page 778)

preach the "good news" (gospel) to all (SALVATION THROUGH JESUS FOR JEWS AND GENTILES, ALIKE!)

Luke 24:47 (page 808)

REPENTANCE & FORGIVENESS OF SINS TO BE PREACHED IN JESUS' NAME TO ALL NATIONS

How does the Great Commission apply to your life?

As a believer, it's my honor & duty to share His gospel

How can you fulfill it in the season of life you are in?

• Demonstrate His love & grace (make Christianity "attractive" to others
• Seize opportunities to tell others

The overriding message of the Gospel of Luke is that nothing is impossible with God. Because of that, Jesus is alive today. Romans 8:34 (page 863) says He is right this minute in the presence of God the Father, interceding for those who believe in Him.

I like the way *The Message* paraphrases it:

> *So, what do you think? With God on our side like this, how can we lose? If God didn't hesitate to put everything on the line for us, embracing our condition and exposing*

himself to the worst by sending his own Son, is there any-
thing else he wouldn't gladly and freely do for us?

And who would dare tangle with God by messing with
one of God's chosen?

Who would dare even to point a finger? The One
who died for us—who was raised to life for us!—is in the
presence of God at this very moment sticking up for us
(Romans 8:31-34 MSG).

Jesus is sticking up for you! That means, as long as you keep your eyes on Him, you cannot lose. He is your Advocate, your Defender, your Protector and, above all, your Savior! If God is for you, who can be against you? (Romans 8:33, page 863). No one! No one that matters because with God on your side, *nothing is impossible!*

 Personal Reflection and Application ———

From this chapter,

I see…

I believe…

I will…

◦◦◦

Prayer

Father, through your Word I see with my own eyes and now testify that you sent your Son to be the Savior of the world. How my spirit rejoices in God my Savior! (1 John 4:14, page 943, and Luke 1:47, page 780).

Thoughts, Notes, and Prayer Requests

Journal Pages

_____

_____

_____

_____

_____

_____

_____

_____

_____

_____

_____

_____

_____

_____

_____

_____

Know God

It does not matter what has happened in your past. No matter what you've done, no matter how you've lived your life,

God is personally interested in you right now.
He cares about you.

God understands your frustration, your loneliness, your heartaches. He wants each of us to come to Him, to know Him personally.

God is so rich in mercy, and he loved us so much, that even
though we were dead because of our sins,
he gave us life when he raised Christ from the dead.
(It is only by God's grace that you have been saved!)
—*Ephesians 2:4-5 (page 895)*

God loves you.

He created you in His image. His desire is to be in relationship with you. He wants you to belong to Him.

Sadly, our sin gets in the way. It separates us from God, and without Him we are dead in our spirits. There is nothing we can do to close that gap. There is nothing we can do to give ourselves life. No matter how well we may behave.

But God loves us so much that He made a way to eliminate that gap and give us new life, His kind of life—to restore the relationship. His love for us is so great, so tremendous, that He sent Jesus Christ, His only Son, to earth to live, and then die—filling the gap and taking the punishment we deserve for refusing God's ways.

God made Christ, who never sinned,
to be the offering for our sin, so that we could
be made right with God through Christ.
—*2 Corinthians 5:21 (page 884)*

Jesus Christ, God's Son, not only died to pay the penalty for your sin, but He conquered death when He rose from the grave. He is ready to share His life with you.

**Christ reconciles us to God. Jesus is alive today.
He will give you a new beginning and a newly created life
when you surrender control of your life to Him.**

Anyone who belongs to Christ has become a new person.
The old life is gone; a new life has begun!
—*2 Corinthians 5:17 (page 884)*

How do you begin this new life? You need to realize

...the necessity of repenting from sin and turning to God,
and of having faith in our Lord Jesus.
—*Acts 20:21 (page 849)*

Agree with God about your sins and believe that Jesus came to save you, that He is your Savior and Lord. Ask Him to lead your life.

God loved the world so much that he gave his one
and only Son, so that everyone who believes in him
will not perish but have eternal life.
God sent his Son into the world not to judge the
world, but to save the world through him.

—John 3:16-17 (page 811)

Pray something like this:

Jesus, I do believe you are the Son of God and that you died on the cross to pay the penalty for my sin. I agree with you about my sin and I want to live a life that pleases you. Enter my life as my Savior and Lord.

I want to follow you and make you the leader of my life.

Thank you for your gift of eternal life and for the Holy Spirit, who has now come to live in me. I ask this in your name. Amen.

God puts His Spirit inside you, who enables you to live a life pleasing to Him. He gives you new life that will never die, that will last forever—eternally.

When you surrender your life to Jesus Christ, you are making the most important decision of your life. Stonecroft would like to offer you a free download of *A New Beginning*, a short Bible study that will help you as you begin your new life in Christ. Go to **stonecroft.org/ newbeginning**.

If you'd like to talk with someone right now about this prayer, call **1.888.NEED.HIM.**

Beginning the Journey
Bible Basics Q & A

The Bible is divided into two sections: the Old Testament (39 books) and the New Testament (27 books). The life of Jesus Christ ties the two together.

What is the Old Testament? The Old Testament contains God's Word that was given to people hundreds of years before Jesus was born on earth. The Bible begins by explaining the creation of the universe and the history of Israel, God's chosen people. This information coincides with archaeology and other sources of recorded history.

What is the New Testament? The New Testament tells us about the life, death, and resurrection of Jesus Christ and describes the experiences of the people He directed to carry on His teachings after He left the earth.

Who is Jesus Christ? *Jesus* means "Savior," and *Christ* means "Messiah" or "Anointed One." Jesus, the Son of God, is God in human form. He proved this truth by living the perfect life, dying on the cross for humanity's sin, and rising from the dead.

What is the connection between the Old Testament and the New Testament? The Old Testament was written before Jesus Christ came to earth. During this time, God communicated to people through prophets and rulers. Many prophecies foretold the coming of Jesus Christ and His activities here on earth. These prophecies were revealed in the Old Testament and fulfilled in the New Testament. More than 300 Old Testament prophecies were fulfilled by Jesus Christ.

How do I look up a Bible verse? The Bible is divided into books, chapters, and verses. When you are asked to look up a verse, it will be in the following format: John 3:16. The name of the Bible book (John) comes first. The first number (3) is the chapter number, and the number following the colon (16) is the verse number.

Why do we study the Bible? The Bible contains more than just concepts that are beneficial for knowledge. Hebrews 4:12 says that "*the Word of God*"—the Bible—"*is alive and powerful.*" That means there is power in the words we read, and the words are applicable to us today just as they were to people thousands of years ago. The Bible aids us in living the way God instructs us to live. We find answers to many of life's difficult questions, wisdom in how to live right, understanding of God's ways, and so much more in God's Word.

How can we make the Bible a part of our lives? The Bible can transform our lives when we not only read it, but put it into practice. When we memorize what it says, its truth is available to us every day and in every situation we face. Psalm 119:11 says, "*I have hidden your word in my heart, that I might not sin against you.*" By keeping God's Word in our hearts, we are able to meditate on its truth and use it as we live out our lives.

Interested in learning more? The Stonecroft Bible Studies *Who Is Jesus?* and *Why Believe?* provide an in-depth look at the person and claims of Jesus Christ.

Who Is Stonecroft?
*Connecting women with God, each other,
and their communities.*

Every day Stonecroft communicates the Gospel in meaningful ways. Whether through a speaker sharing her transformational story, or side by side in a ministry service project, the Gospel of Jesus Christ goes forward. In one-on-one conversations with a long-term friend, and through well-developed online and print resources, the Gospel of Jesus Christ goes forward.

For nearly 75 years, we've been introducing women to Jesus Christ and training them to share His Good News with others.

Stonecroft understands and appreciates the influence of one woman's life. When you reach her, you touch everyone she knows—her family, friends, neighbors, and co-workers. The real Truth of the Gospel brings real redemption into real lives.

Our life-changing, faith-building community resources include:

- ***Stonecroft Bible and Book Studies***—both topical and traditional chapter-by-chapter studies. Stonecroft studies are designed for those in small groups—those who know Christ and those who do not yet know Him—to simply yet profoundly discover God's Word together.

- ***Outreach Events and Service Activities***—set the stage for women to be encouraged and equipped to hear and share the Gospel with their communities. Whether in a large venue, workshop, or small group setting, women are prepared to serve their communities with the love of Christ.

- *Small Group Studies for Christians*—these studies engage believers in God's heart for those who do not know Him. Our most recent, the Aware Series, includes *Aware, Belong,* and *Call.*

- *Stonecroft Life Publications*—clearly explain the Gospel through stories of people whose lives have been transformed by Jesus Christ.

- *Stonecroft Prayer*—foundational for everything we do, prayer groups, materials, and training set the focus on our reliance on God for all ministry and to share the Gospel.

- *Stonecroft's Website*—stonecroft.org—offering fresh content daily to equip and encourage you.

Dedicated and enthusiastic Stonecroft staff serve you via Divisional Field Directors stationed across the United States, and a Home Office team overseeing the leadership of tens of thousands of dedicated volunteers worldwide.

Your life matters. Join us today to impact your communities with the Gospel of Jesus Christ. Become involved with Stonecroft.

To get started, visit us at **stonecroft.org** or contact us via **connections@stonecroft.org** or **800.525.8627**.

STONECROFT

stonecroft.org

Books for Further Study

Bock, Darrell L. *Luke*. The NIV Application Commentary. Grand Rapids, MI: Zondervan, 1996.

Chan, Francis. *Crazy Love*. Colorado Springs, CO: David C. Cook, 2008.

Idleman, Kyle. *not a fan*. Grand Rapids, MI: Zondervan, 2011.

Morgan, Elisa. *She Did What She Could*. Colorado Springs, CO: Tyndale House Publishing, 2009.

Pfeiffer, Charles F., and Everett Harrison. *The Wycliffe Bible Commentary*. Chicago, IL: Moody Press, 1962.

Stott, John R.W. *Basic Christianity*. Downers Grove, IL: Inter-Varsity Press, 2006.

Stonecroft Resources

Stonecroft Bible Studies make the Word of God accessible to everyone. These studies allow small groups to discover the adventure of a personal relationship with God and introduce others to God's unlimited love, grace, forgiveness, and power. To learn more, visit stonecroft.org/biblestudies.

Who Is Jesus? (6 chapters)
He was a rebel against the status quo. The religious community viewed Him as a threat. The helpless and outcast considered Him a friend. Explore the life and teachings of Jesus—this rebel with a cause who challenges us today to a life of radical faith.

What Is God Like? (6 chapters)
What is God like? Is He just a higher power? Has He created us and left us on our own? Where is He when things don't make sense? Discover what the Bible tells us about God and how we can know Him in a life-transforming way.

Who Is the Holy Spirit? (6 chapters)
Are you living up to the full life that God has for you? Learn about the Holy Spirit, our Helper and power source for everyday living, who works in perfect harmony with God the Father and Jesus the Son.

Connecting with God (8 chapters)
Prayer is our heart-to-heart communication with our heavenly Father. This study examines the purpose, power, and elements of prayer, sharing biblical principles for effective prayer.

Today I Pray

When we bow before God on behalf of someone who doesn't yet know of His saving work, of His great love in sending His Son Jesus, of His mercy and goodness, we enter into a work that has eternal impact. Stonecroft designed *Today I Pray* as a 30-day intercessory prayer commitment that you may use to focus your prayers on behalf of a specific person, or to pray for many—because your prayers are powerful and important!

Prayer Worth Repeating (15 devotions)

There is no place where your prayers to the one and only God cannot penetrate, no circumstance prayers cannot impact. As the mother of adult children, your greatest influence into their lives is through prayer. *Prayer Worth Repeating* is a devotional prayer guide designed to focus your prayers and encourage you to trust God more deeply as He works in the lives of your adult children.

Pray & Play Devotional (12 devotions)

It's playgroup with a purpose! Plus Mom tips. For details on starting a Pray & Play group, visit stonecroft.org/prayandplay or call 800.525.8627.

Prayer Journal

A practical resource to strengthen your prayer life, this booklet includes an introductory section about the importance of prayer, the basic elements of prayer and a clear Gospel presentation, as well as 40 pages of journaling your prayer requests and God's answers.

Prayer—Talking with God

This booklet provides insight and biblical principles to help you establish a stronger, more effective prayer life.

Aware (5 lessons)

Making Jesus known every day starts when we are *Aware* of those around us. This dynamic Stonecroft Small Group Bible Study about "Always Watching And Responding with Encouragement" equips and engages people in the initial steps to the joys of evangelism.

Belong (6 lessons)

For many in today's culture, the desire to belong is often part of their journey to believe. *Belong* explores how we can follow in Jesus' footsteps—and walk with others on their journey to belong.

Call (7 lessons)

Every day we meet people without Christ. That is God's intention.

He wants His people to initiate and build friendships. He wants us together. *Call* helps us take a closer look at how God makes Himself known through our relationships with those around us.

Discover together God's clear calling for you and those near to you.

These and many more Stonecroft resources are available to you. Order today to impact your communities with the Gospel of Jesus Christ. Simply visit **stonecroft.org/store** to get started.

If you have been encouraged and brought closer to God by this study, please consider giving a gift to Stonecroft so that others can experience life change as well. You can find information about giving online at **stonecroft.org**. (Click on the "Donate" tab.)

If you'd like to give via telephone, please contact us at **800.525.8627.** Or you can mail your gift to

Stonecroft
PO Box 9609
Kansas City, MO 64134-0609

STONECROFT

PO Box 9609, Kansas City, MO 64134-0609
Telephone: 816.763.7800 | 800.525.8627
E-mail: connections@stonecroft.org | stonecroft.org

Abundant Life Bible
New Living Translation Holy Bible

Experience the presence of God in everyday life

Stonecroft is pleased to partner with Tyndale to offer the New Living Translation Holy Bible as the companion for our newly released Stonecroft Bible Studies.

The New Living Translation translators set out to render the message of the original Scripture language texts into clear, contemporary English. In this *translation*, scholars kept the concerns of both formal-equivalence and dynamic-equivalence in mind. Their goal was a Bible that is faithful to the ancient texts and eminently readable. The result is a translation that is both accurate and powerful.

TRUTH MADE CLEAR

Features of the Abundant Life Bible

- Features are easy-to-use and written for people who don't yet know Jesus Christ personally.
- Unequaled clarity and accuracy
- Dictionary included
- Concordance included
- Old Testament included

- Introductory notes on important abundant life topics such as:
  Gospel presentation   Practical guidance
  Joy   Life's tough issues
  Peace   Prayer
- Insights from a relationship with Jesus Christ.
- Ideal Scripture text for those not familiar with the Bible!

 Tyndale House Publishers

To order: stonecroft.org/store
800.525.8627

 STONECROFT
stonecroft.org/SBS

Notes

1. This paragraph and the following, through the bullet points, are quoted or adapted from Earle L. Wingo, *The Illegal Trial of Jesus* (New York: Charter Books/Bobbs-Merrill Co. Inc., 1954), pages 29, 47-48.

2. Paul L. Maier, "The Empty Tomb as History," *Christianity Today*, March 1975, pp. 4-6.